Praise for
HR You Kidding Me?

Cory Sanford offers a fresh new approach to developing people in organizations. His book is funny, engaging, inspiring, and delightfully well written. He teaches us to "think big, start small" with dozens of tips we can apply right now. It is a must read for executives, managers, HR directors, and anyone who works with people. If you want to win a "Best Place to Work" award, order copies of the book and have your whole team read it.

Michael Glauser | Executive Director, Center for Entrepreneurship, Utah State University | Author of *One People One Planet* and *Main Street Entrepreneur*

As a leadership professor at Boise State University, a seasoned consultant, and author of three leadership books, I've seen it all. But Cory Sanford's *HR You Kidding Me?* blew me away. He masterfully weaves captivating stories and leadership principles with impactful HR practices, offering a game-changer for team management. My own approach has been fundamentally reshaped thanks to Sanford's brilliance.

Dr. Jeremy Graves | Professor, Boise State University, | Executive Leadership Coach | Author of *The Leader Paradox* and *Leading Across Generations*

An entertaining journey through the field of human resources, packed with practical tips and tools for anyone who manages people.

Bradford S. Bell | William J. Conaty Professor of Strategic Human Resources and Director, Center for Advanced Human Resource Studies, Cornell University

Managing people is both the most fulfilling and frustrating part of running a business. Cory, and the concepts in his book, will help you minimize and eliminate these frustrations so you can focus on the fulfilling part: developing your team to their full potential. The majority of HR professionals excel either at administration or at nurturing culture, rarely both. Cory shatters this norm. His mastery lies in formulating simple yet effective frameworks for standardizing HR practices, reducing complexities and achieving objectives without fostering red tape. I can attest that his methods have helped us make HR administration much easier, while also amplifying the engagement, connection, and contribution of our team members. Among many other relevant topics in his book, he shares the experiences and insights he gathered as we transitioned a US team in one office to a fully remote global organization with team members in 6 countries and 14 US States. I have no doubt you will find multiple nuggets in this book that will deliver a high ROI for the time you invest to read it.

Jeremy Ames | CEO & Co-founder, Guidant Financial

Human Resources professionals should not miss the opportunity to read *HR You Kidding Me?* by Cory Sanford. Through the pages of this book, Cory's passion for people and the purpose of HR is palpable. He expertly navigates readers through the complex components of HR, providing entertaining and humorous examples that will leave readers feeling equipped to tackle the numerous responsibilities associated with the field.

Cory values culture and the importance of connections, and his personal stories and examples throughout the book make it easy to connect with him, his family, and his co-workers. *HR You Kidding Me?* is not only a valuable resource for existing HR professionals but can also inspire others to pursue a career in HR.

Michelle Beauchamp | Founder/CEO of The Champ Group, Author of *Relearn Leadership*

So many books are filled with technical jargon and ideas that have not been tested. Those who read *HR You Kidding Me?* will find it practical, thought provoking, and easily applicable to ACTUAL real-world situations. The book is an actionable workbook that can be used instantly, regardless of organization or experience. Cory offers a pragmatic and practical perspective. Whether you are just getting started or you are a veteran practitioner we can all benefit from a refreshing perspective on how to practically improve our function and the organizations we support. I have had the pleasure of working with and knowing Cory for many years and this book keeps with his personal style - practical, engaging, and grounded in real world experiences.

Matthew D Owenby | Chief Strategy Officer and Corporate Services Executive, Aflac Inc.

I am honored to endorse Cory's book, a treasure trove of wisdom and guidance that encapsulates the invaluable lessons I've had the privilege to learn during our five years working together at Guidant. Cory's mentorship has been a gift, and his ability to simplify complex concepts while providing the space for personal discovery and growth is nothing short of remarkable. Through his insights and infectious optimism, he encourages readers to ask the right questions, fostering an environment of continuous learning. This book is a reflection of Cory's unique ability to build long-lasting relationships, genuinely care for others, and inspire impactful change. As I reflect on my own experiences under Cory's guidance, I am confident that this book will serve as a powerful tool for individuals seeking to make a meaningful impact in their businesses and the lives they touch.

Laura Paradis, PHR | People Program Manager, Guidant Financial

Cory Sanford's vision for HR is both inspiring and practical, a rare find in business literature. This book is an invaluable resource for anyone looking to create a positive organizational change.

Shawn Johal | Business Growth Coach, Elevation Leaders, Bestselling Author of *The Happy Leader*

After reading *HR You Kidding Me?*, I feel newly equipped to tackle HR challenges. Sanford's book offers a unique blend of strategies that are both insightful and actionable, changing the way I approach HR.

Sanjay Jaybhay | Author of *Invest and Grow Rich*

Cory Sanford's book is a must-read for modern HR professionals. It's filled with cutting-edge strategies and real-world examples that have transformed how I think about my team.

Tamara Nall | CEO & Founder, The Leading Niche

HR You Kidding Me? is a standout read in the HR field. Cory Sanford's practical solutions to traditional HR challenges are essential for today's business leaders.

Dr. Kathy Humel | CEO, Senior Consultant RxKHumel, LLC

DO YOU WANT TO BE THE BEST LEADER YOUR TEAM HAS EVER HAD?

It's time to make your greatest impact.

While true perfection in leadership is as elusive as a silver bullet, mastering one-on-one meetings with your team can be your closest bet. This self-assessment tool is your gateway to mastering this critical skill.

- Assess the impact of your one-on-one engagement
- Identify leadership strengths and opportunities for growth
- Set a trajectory for your professional development
- Gain actionable insights to drive your team's success

Download your free one-on-one meeting self-assessment tool:

and begin the journey that will elevate your leadership and shape your future success.

Read Chapter 11: The Silver Bullet in Leadership* to learn more.

HR You Kidding Me?

Surprisingly Simple Steps to Unlock the Power of People

Leaders
Press

CORY SANFORD

Leaders
Press

ISBN 978-1-63735-242-7 (pbk)
ISBN 978-1-63735-243-4 (ebook)

Library of Congress Control Number: 2023924589

This book is dedicated to the amazing leaders who have mentored me and given me the space to safely learn, fail, grow, and now share the wonderful experiences we had together: Bethany Calley, Jason and Keith Fletcher, David Nilssen, and Jeremy Ames.

Table of Contents

SECTION 4: Sharpening Human Resources Tools

SECTION 5: What's Next?

Foreword

The modern challenges that businesses face today are far more complex than they were a decade ago. As the CEO of Guidant Financial, when I first met Cory Sanford, we were transitioning from a centralized business in Bellevue, WA, to a decentralized operation, eventually spanning fourteen states and six countries. From this experience, I came to deeply respect Cory's expertise, as well as buy into his vision.

The onset of COVID-19 added a layer of complexity to our plans. The decision to transition Guidant Financial to a fully remote workforce was ambitious. Cory was instrumental in helping us pivot from our renowned in-office experience to a celebrated remote culture. It's a testament to him that in 2023, we were recognized as the #1 Best Place to Work in Idaho—the only fully remote organization to be so honored.

Cory's genius transcends borders. As his book title *HR You Kidding Me?* implies, he confronts the role of conventional Human Resources and challenges us to strive for the extraordinary. His insights emphasize that the workplace should be an oasis where individuals thrive, a place where they not only contribute their best but also derive energy that enhances their personal lives. This vision resonates with every leader who aspires to cultivate an environment where employees feel invigorated and empowered.

Diving deep into HR, Cory outlines how the profession has evolved over time—from a department mainly concerned with administrative duties to one that plays a pivotal role in driving the strategic goals of organizations. And it's not just about changing HR's approach but also about altering our perceptions. For example, he advocates that HR should embrace the idea of helping people to solve their own problems. It's about empowering, fostering autonomy, and ensuring every individual feels confident to voice their concerns and seek resolutions.

Drawing from my own experience, Cory's support and insights were instrumental when I ventured into establishing Doxa Talent, as we scaled from 10 employees to a whopping 750 in just two years. Cory's mastery lies in his ability to strike that perfect balance—protecting the organization, nurturing its people, advocating for workers' rights, and fostering a powerful culture of connection that all align to meet inspiring organizational outcomes.

The chapters of *HR You Kidding Me?* serve as a roadmap, guiding us through the most basic aspects of HR, from the essentials of the employee life cycle to the nuances of transforming culture, leadership dynamics, and fine-tuning HR tools. *The Future Is Borderless®*, so any executive with ambitions of leading in this new era must embrace the wisdom encapsulated in this book.

HR You Kidding Me? is a blueprint for any organization aiming to foster a world-class culture. The challenges of tomorrow demand innovative solutions, and Cory provides the strategies, inspirations, and tools necessary to navigate the future, which is already here and still evolving.

–David Nilssen
Co-founder of Guidant Financial and CEO, Doxa Talent

Preface

During morning recess one day when I was six years old, in first grade, I was playing on the monkey bars with a friend. I was trying to see how high I could swing my feet forward and backward. As I was swinging backward, I slipped and fell hard to the ground, placing my hands down first to catch my fall and protect my face. It was scary, and it hurt. My friend from class, Ben, also only six years old, knelt next to me and asked if I was okay. I told him my wrists hurt really bad. He immediately suggested we talk to the ground duty; he helped me up and led the way.

When we got to the ground duty—easy to spot in her bright orange vest designed to be highly visible for just such an occasion—Ben explained what happened. She looked at me, held up one of my wrists, and told me that because I wasn't crying, I couldn't be hurt that bad. The bell rang, and she directed me to go back to class.

When I got back to Mr. Sessions's first-grade class, Ben and I told him the story. Mr. Sessions told me he thought I was trying to get out of the spelling test and instructed me to sit down and get ready for the test. I could no longer grip a pencil properly, so I completed the spelling test by holding the pencil in between my wrists. (If you're able to right now, try it—it's hard!).

At lunch, Ben and I talked to Janitor Bob (that's how he introduced himself). He made delicious suckers at home in different shapes, colors, and flavors and sold them to kids at school for a quarter. For many reasons, I don't think this would happen today! We had a good relationship, as he regularly satisfied my cinnamon-flavored, star-shaped sucker cravings. He listened to our story, and while I could tell he cared, he said that he was "just a janitor" and that I needed to go to the office since my teacher didn't listen.

So two six-year-olds walked to the elementary school's principal's office. We were so short that the secretary had to stand up and peer over the counter to see us. For the fourth time that day, we explained what happened. As she was responding that she didn't think anything was wrong, the principal came out of her office because she overheard the conversation. She asked if I cried. When I told her no, she told me to eat lunch and not do monkey bars anymore that day.

I normally walked to and from school. Because I had an appointment after school that day, my mom picked me up. I was unable to open the car door because my wrists didn't have the strength to make that lifting motion and it caused a lot of pain. I tried several times before my mom opened the door for me and asked what was wrong. I told her, "I fell off the monkey bars and hurt my wrists, but all the adults told me I was okay." She looked at my wrists, saw the swelling, and took me straight to the doctor for X-rays.

The result: two broken wrists.

I went to school the next day with two casts that surprised the adults I had spoken to the day before. I'll always remember the choice words, which I won't repeat here, that my dad had for the principal when he showed her my two broken arms.

None of the adults at the school got on my level physically or emotionally to understand what I was experiencing. I told this story because it reflects a fundamental problem in Human Resources (HR). I know what it's like to believe in something and face hurdles, doubt, and disappointment along the way. I've experienced the roller coaster of being very motivated to make a positive impact and then being discouraged because of how hard it can be to find sound and practical guidance. Working in HR and as a people leader is both the most challenging and most fulfilling work I have ever done. I absolutely love working in HR and taking this leadership journey with people like you.

As you read this book, I hope you will see a lot of common ground and similarities in our experiences and feelings. I have learned a lot over fifteen great years in Human Resources and helping two different companies earn #1 Best Place to Work award-winning honors. I'm excited to share what's worked for me when facing the various challenges and opportunities we have in our roles.

I believe the workplace should be an environment where people can be their best, do their best, and feel their best. Instead of jobs draining energy, my vision is for work to be a place where people come to contribute and gain energy to take back to personal lives to be the best partners, parents, coaches, volunteers, musicians, or any other role that is meaningful.

I wrote this book for the person in the small company where people are wearing many hats, including the Human Resources function, for the brand-new supervisor, and for experienced HR and business leaders alike. There is something for everyone.

In *The Little Book of Leadership*, Jeffrey Gitomer writes, "This is NOT a book for you to read and say, 'I know that.' This book will challenge you to ask yourself, 'How good am I at that?'"[1] As you read this book with that same perspective, I hope you have four experiences:

1. Feel empowered and confident to try something new from over one hundred different practical tips and become inspired to be part of a large group that is trying to get better every day in

leadership and Human Resources roles.

2. Feel validated and celebrated for the great work you are already doing, especially when you read something in the book that's working well for you.

3. Have fun. I hope you enjoy the book enough to have some new stories and examples to think about, laugh about, and apply in different ways. Laughter accelerates learning.

4. Have a desire to reach out to me—I want to know what works for you, what you've tried that didn't go as you expected, and I am always a fan of funny stories. Send them to HRYouKiddingMe@gmail.com or let's connect on LinkedIn: https://www.linkedin.com/in/Cory-Sanford.

Because I'll be referencing my work experience throughout the book, here is a quick synopsis:

- Ada County. Local government that includes Boise, Idaho's capital.

- Ashley Manor and Auburn Crest Home Health and Hospice. Large healthcare group with assisted living and memory care communities, along with home health and hospice offices, with sixty-five total locations in four states.

- Guidant Financial. Tech-enabled finance company that specializes in small business success by offering financing, payroll, bookkeeping, and tax services.

- Cornell University. A world-class university in New York State. I am an instructor in the Executive Masters of Human Resource Management program.

- tHRee60 Consulting. Founder and chief excitement officer offering consulting, training workshops, coaching, and keynote presentations.

While I hope you read and enjoy the entire book, feel free to read straight through or after reading the "Introduction: Think Big, Start Small," take a *Choose Your Own Adventure*-style approach and jump to chapters that are most relevant for you.

Let's go have some fun!

Introduction

Think big, start small.

I was tempted to end the introduction there to prove a point. Instead, I'll add a little context.

As an instructor in Cornell University's Executive Master of Human Resource Management program, I once hosted a live discussion with a cohort comprising some of the brightest and most successful Human Resources professionals I've ever met.

As our great conversation evolved from the course topic of talent management to the ambitious projects and responsibilities these leaders were working on, they seemed simultaneously excited and exhausted.

I told them something that I learned the hard way was, "Think big, start small." Silence. Then awareness, profound relief, smiles and laughter, and note-taking. Several of the students told me later that this alone was "worth the price of admission" and "something I really needed to hear—and need to hear often." It was as if they needed to permit themselves to slow down, be thoughtful, and enjoy the journey—as ambitious, smart, successful people often do. I'm also giving you permission (you're welcome). Will you give yourself permission?

I can certainly relate to needing to hear this often, as I seem to learn this lesson again and again the hard way. We want to boil the ocean, eat the elephant, have a grand adventure, make a profound positive impact, or whichever metaphor you want to use. It all must start with a single pot of water, one bite, one step, and one person at a time.

A couple of years ago, I submitted my ten-year notice of resignation. I have big plans after that, so I'm taking some small steps to get there. It felt good!

For this book, I have big dreams. I wrote this "Introduction" first on purpose. I needed the personal reminder right out of the gate that while I hope to make a tremendous difference in the work experience for you and those you lead, I can enjoy the process of writing each sentence, paragraph, and chapter.

Human Resources has many exciting and fulfilling elements: seeing people grow, advance, succeed, achieve, earn more, contribute more, innovate, create, enjoy their work, and develop meaningful relations with teammates and clients. I hope you as the reader will find inspiration and confidence to think big, with some immediate practical tools to start small, and ultimately achieve your big dreams.

SECTION 1

Employee Life Cycle

The Role of Human Resources

Toby Flenderson.

That name alone probably evokes some different emotions and reactions from those who recognize the name as the Human Resources professional on the successful NBC show, *The Office*. The show intended Flenderson to evoke laughter, awkwardness, anger, and suspicion. Here is how Michael Scott, the lead character in the show played by Steve Carrell, describes Toby at various points throughout the series: Jerky McJerkface, Waste of Life, The Worst, Satan, The Antichrist, Evil Snail, and Everything Wrong with the Paper Industry. In possibly the meanest insult in sitcom history, Michael once said, "If I had a gun with two bullets, and I was in a room with Hitler, Bin Laden, and Toby, I would shoot Toby twice."[1]

I know Human Resources professionals who are offended by the way we are portrayed in shows, and I know many people who believe we deserve to be portrayed in this manner. Still, I know more people like me who choose to laugh and see it as an opportunity for all of us to prove them wrong by making great contributions to organizations and the work experience.

Have you been on LinkedIn lately (or ever)? There is always lots of noise and debate about the role and benefits (or negatives) of Human Resources. While I don't dwell on this, it fuels a fire in me to want to stand out and make a positive impact.

Here are some companies that try to answer "What is the role of Human Resources?"

- According to Paycor: "(P)rovide organizational structure and the ability to meet business needs by effectively managing the employee life cycle."[2]
- According to Indeed: "(M)anage the concerns and needs that relate to the human capital of the organization."[3]

I'll occasionally use this exercise with senior leadership groups or Human Resources teams.

- First, I'll ask them to describe the Human Resources function in one sentence.
- Next, I'll ask them to describe the Human Resources function in three words.
- Last, I'll ask them to describe the Human Resources function in one word.

Because I'm writing this in the middle of a surge of artificial intelligence growth, I asked ChatGPT these questions. Here is the response describing the Human Resources function:

- In one sentence: Optimizing workforce efficiency, development, and well-being while

ensuring compliance with organizational policies and legal requirements.
- In three words: Recruitment, Training, Management.
- In one word: People.[4]

Let's pause here. I think it's important for you to reflect on these questions to see what your perspectives and feelings are. If you're a supervisor and not part of a Human Resources team, you might ask yourself these questions as they relate to your role with the people on your team.

There are multiple right answers, so going through these exercises makes them even more helpful. Here are a couple of examples of how I think about the role of Human Resources:

"Aligning people in an organization to win together."

I also like "Stewards of culture that maximize talent to achieve positive business impacts."

Whenever people ask what I do for work, I tell them that I am the vice president of culture and talent for an awesome company where my job is to make sure everyone loves their jobs.

This is a very different perspective from Michael Scott's in *The Office*. What is your favorite definition of the role of Human Resources?

This exercise can bring visibility into where people are aligned and where there might be a need for more alignment. Despite there being multiple great ways to define the function, this visibility and definition can bring important clarity and excitement. I've learned a few lessons over the years that can help all of us approach our roles with more clarity. Each section below is an example of how we can we can understand the role of HR and maximize our impact.

Guide the Employee Life Cycle

Let's be experts in the employee life cycle. I use the tool below when discussing Human Resources management. It's fluid and leaves room for additional thoughts at each step. The important points are that the actions of a United States company are guided by federal laws, then state/local laws, then company policy and culture. This order is critical because actions can only get more employee-friendly. For example, as of this writing, federal laws do not require paid time off, some states might require at least one week of sick leave, and a company might offer two weeks of sick leave. Notice how each became more favorable to an employee.

Additionally, I think the main categories of the employee life cycle are standard: Recruitment, Selection, Onboarding, Performance Management, Promotion, Offboarding. Many different activities are possible within those steps. Some activities are required by law, others by company policy; some might be best practices, and others might be unique to your organization or industry. Chapters throughout this book speak to different elements of the employee life cycle, with my experience and perspective on getting the best results.

Finally, these steps are supported by a variety of different tools to help create effectiveness and efficiency. We aren't required to have many of these tools by federal or state regulations—rather, we deploy them to improve the employee life cycle and our impact as we guide team members through each step.

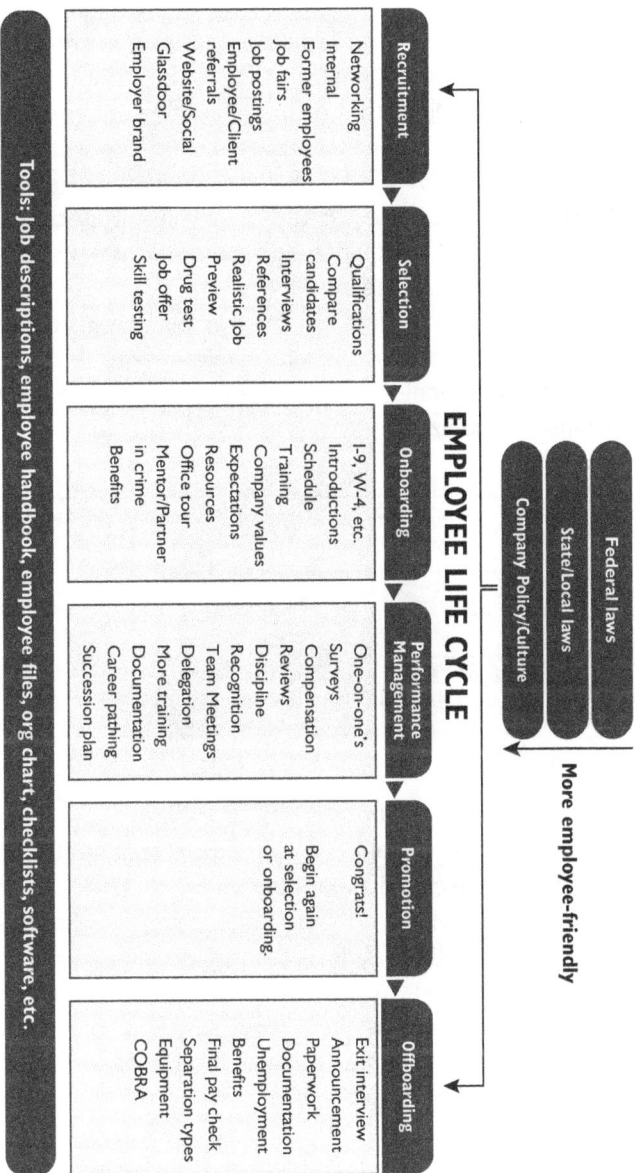

EMPLOYEE LIFE CYCLE

Recruitment	Selection	Onboarding	Performance Management	Promotion	Offboarding
Networking	Qualifications	I-9, W-4, etc.	One-on-one's	Congrats!	Exit interview
Internal	Compare candidates	Introductions	Surveys	Begin again at selection or onboarding.	Announcement
Former employees	Interviews	Schedule	Compensation		Paperwork
Job fairs	References	Training	Reviews		Documentation
Job postings	Realistic Job Preview	Company values	Discipline		Unemployment
Employee/Client referrals	Drug test	Expectations	Recognition		Benefits
Website/Social	Job offer	Resources	Team Meetings		Final pay check
Glassdoor	Skill testing	Office tour	Delegation		Separation types
Employer brand		Mentor/Partner in crime	More training		Equipment
		Benefits	Documentation		COBRA
			Career pathing		
			Succession plan		

Company Policy/Culture

State/Local laws

Federal laws

More employee-friendly

Tools: job descriptions, employee handbook, employee files, org chart, checklists, software, etc.

Scope and Impact

Here is a graphic I created to demonstrate the progress of Human Resources. First, the Personnel department was created to help with short-term, administrative work, mostly centered around compliance and organization of information. Over the last few decades, Human Resources has expanded to add more value strategically and long term while still managing the important short-term administrative needs.

Our goal is for HR to fill this box by being trusted by all business leaders to leverage talent, expertise, and relationships to achieve the long-term strategic goals of the whole organization.

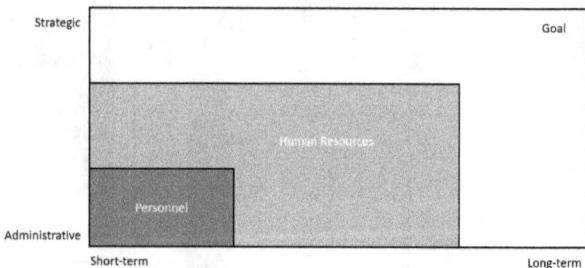

Different organizations will be at different places on this chart. Where, in your opinion, is your organization?

I know some organizations where the chief HR officer is being prepared for, or has been promoted to, the CEO role. I'd say they've done a good job of maximizing the strategic, long-term elements of the function. I also spoke with someone last week where the CEO of a small start-up wants to eliminate most of the HR department. He doesn't see the benefits of HR.

I think the value here is to recognize our goal and our potential. It's also helpful to acknowledge where we fall within our organization. I hope this will help motivate us to find ways to streamline the short-term administrative functions so we can spend more time on the people and strategies that will make significant long-term contributions. (See "Chapter 12: E.A.S.E. into More Effectiveness.")

I really like that ChatGPT summarized Human Resources with one word: *people*. As the role has grown, we've seen a shift in language from Personnel to Human Resources to People, Talent, or Culture. I'm open to all three of the latter options, provided we're meeting the long-term strategies of the organization through our work.

Put Ourselves Out of a Job

I thought that heading might get your attention.

Let me explain: I think we need to be working to develop people and processes so well that we put ourselves out of a job. We should consistently ask ourselves: "How do we set up an organization to function phenomenally without us?"

I know that probably sounds scary for some people and may earn an "Amen!" from our critics. Because it seems that our instinct is often to create job security through dependencies on our knowledge instead of working hard to set up an organization for success without us. In the book *Turn the Ship Around,* which is about a U.S. Navy submarine, David Marquet points out a common problem, "Officers are rewarded for being indispensable, for being missed after they depart. When the performance of a unit goes down after an officer leaves, it is taken as a sign that he was a good leader, not (as a sign) that he was ineffective in training his people properly."[5] This is at the beginning of the book. Marquet spends the rest of the book describing how we can set organizations up for success that survives individual leaders.

There is greater satisfaction in empowering others for their long-term individual success and the long-term success of the organization. The exciting irony is that, if you can find a way to develop people and processes so well that it puts you out of a job, there will always be work for you to do, probably at the same company. That skill set is priceless. Jeremy Ames, CEO at Guidant Financial told me, "People that can replace themselves are irreplaceable."

Focusing on putting ourselves out of a job creates the right attitude and mindset to be creative, take some risks, and think much larger and much further into the future.

Support the Organizational Structure

If I had written "Support the chain of command" for the title of this section, I am confident some people would react with, "I knew it! HR only exists to protect the company!"

I prefer the term *organizational structure* because I think "command" is outdated and misaligned with the cultures of many organizations, and because I like to think of the company as a building or a structure. In this case, support of a structure means to develop and reinforce, not necessarily to agree all the time.

So when I say that a key role of Human Resources is to support the organizational structure, I mean that HR is an internally focused function and that we let company leaders be company leaders.

I'll explain both:

When I joined a healthcare company, I worked hard to develop good relationships with everybody, including the people in our home office who I saw every day. After some discussions, presentations, and meetings, some people concluded that I was a person who they could trust. Yes! The problem was, when clients would call into our home office upset about a billing issue or confusion about their loved one's care, these same employees thought that I would be a good person to talk to them. One person came to my office and asked if I would talk to a customer. I politely told them no. They were surprised. I explained that all I could do was listen and that I wasn't in a position to solve their problem. This is a major disservice to them. Customers who want to escalate a concern can do so through the operational organization structure or finance organizational structure (depending upon the issue), all the way up to the CEO. When I explained this, I suggested they find out who this person had talked to about their concern so far, and to help connect them with the next person up in the organization. At the time, each assisted living home had a licensed administrator who reported to a director of operations, who reported to a vice president, who reported to the CEO. All much better people than a member of the Human Resources team for understanding and being able to resolve questions about contracts, payments, services, regulations, care needs, etc.

The next part of supporting the organizational structure may spark some debate among HR professionals and company leaders. I firmly believe that our role is to support the company leaders by preparing them to have all the necessary conversations with their team members. That includes progressive discipline, compensation, promotion, terminations, and so on. Both the fun moments and the challenging ones. As a leader, it can be hard sometimes to see the forest for the trees. Having a trusted HR resource can be an advantage in understanding policies, context, history, and culture, which then helps the leader to perform their leadership responsibilities.

I am aware of some organizations where the HR team members attend, and sometimes lead, all conversations with employees. Because I believe so strongly that the most important relationship at work is with the person's direct supervisor and that strong relationships are built by having both fun and challenging conversations, I believe it is the responsibility of HR to work with supervisors to prepare them to successfully lead those conversations on their own. This preparation could be data, a talk script, or a mock meeting where they practice. Let's work hard to get people to be effective and confident. Having an HR professional in every employee meeting doesn't scale, and it limits the growth and effectiveness of the leader. That's what I mean when I say *support* the organizational structure. Even though we might think that we would do a better job during a progressive discipline conversation, or we might find it rewarding to attend a meeting where someone is being promoted, that is the role of the leader. Even though it might be more work to do it this way in the beginning, this is the long-term view we need to take for the success of that leader and the organization.

Let's help leaders get the credit for the great conversations and see the satisfaction of navigating a more challenging situation.

Help People to Solve Their Own Problems

This one is hard because we often love to be problem solvers. With a few exceptions (such as severe accusations of harassment or discrimination), my philosophy is "I don't fix people's problems, I help people solve their own problems." HR's role is to support the organizational structure, ask thought-provoking questions, provide tools, and encourage communication. We must be careful not to undermine management authority by taking on the causes of employees or doing their job for them—which often involves having a conversation with another person or tracking down information.

Here are a couple of examples:

- A manager emails a question about bereavement leave that is in the employee handbook. I might answer the question in the email, include a link to the handbook, and if they want additional information, encourage them to check out the page about bereavement in the handbook. I hope this empowers them to first seek information there the next time they have a policy question.
- An employee feels their supervisor isn't being fair about approving time off. Let's help that employee feel comfortable and confident enough to bring their concern directly to that supervisor.

Culture Stewards

One of the most important roles in HR is representing the culture of an organization. Here are some ways we can best do this:

- Learn (memorize!) company values and principles. Live them the very best we can.
- Recognize others when they live them and specifically mention the value or principle in that recognition, and reference values and principles in dialogue and decision-making.

- Include culture champions in interview panels when seeking feedback on company decisions, and on committees that help promote company culture.
- Solicit feedback from the team on where the culture, values, and principles are being lived well in the organization and where improvement is needed.
- Bring energy and support to all activities designed to create connections.

One secret weapon: thank-you cards. Gratitude is an unlimited social and emotional currency. The more we give, the better we and others feel. Let's set the example of expressing gratitude for accomplishments, effort, living values, when someone chooses to join the team, or even when someone gets a great job outside of our company.

Not sure yet that there's a need? Think about how great it feels to receive a thank-you note. Most people display them at their desk for years because they have become too rare. Ask your payroll person how often they get thank-you cards for making sure everyone gets paid accurately and on time multiple times per month. That's a great place to start.

Learn the Business

Whatever our business, it is our responsibility to learn it. Yes, there is so much to accomplish and ways to grow just within our Human Resources and/or leadership responsibilities. We will achieve the most when we understand the business well enough to apply the principles of HR and leadership to it.

Attend industry conferences, speak to operations people as high up in the organization as you can, visit the factories or call centers or locations where your organization operates, lean into opportunities to make business decisions, understand financial statements, and read relevant news articles. Let's be business leaders first who happen to be highly skilled human resources professionals.

In one organization, I volunteered to manage our social media accounts, overhaul our website, and update our branding. This experience allowed me to better leverage the way we recruited. I also led efforts to create an intranet (we used Dropbox) to centralize, standardize, and make accessible the most current documents for the whole company. We used this to publish a lot of company-wide and operational data. We also had high leverage for Human Resources information. We could publish policies, job descriptions, benefits materials, training, etc. Notice how contributing to company-wide projects created direct benefits for HR functions.

We have a lot of work to do! I hope this helps to simplify and clarify some of the ways we can discipline ourselves to make the most long-term positive impact on our organizations and team members.

After giving this chapter some thought, how would you briefly define the role of Human Resources? Write it below and let's get to it!

_____

_____

_____

_____

2

Hiring for Culture 1—Start Selection with Reflection

I had a friend in my high school biology class who failed the final project to grow a sunflower plant. We had all year to water and nurture our potted seeds, and he still didn't get anything to grow.

When he presented his plantless pot to the class, the teacher asked, "What kind of seed did you use?"

"Barbecue," he said.

He tried to grow a sunflower plant from baked barbecue-flavored sunflower seeds. He thought that all seeds were the same and it was easier to get seeds from his pantry instead of a store, not realizing that cooking and seasoning sunflower seeds kills any germination potential.

Even though I laugh every time I think about that, there is an important lesson: You can't burn a seed and then expect it to thrive. It matters what seeds we choose to grow.

Let's apply this to recruiting. Each person we select for our company can grow and contribute significantly, or they could not be the right fit and some cause organizational damage before either party realizes it.

I've seen poor-fit hires drive away high performers, with companies inadvertently trading top production for lower production.

There are likely many of us who have had the experience of hiring someone who didn't work out as we hoped. We've also likely had, from both sides of the hiring table, some very interesting experiences with the whole hiring process. When I worked at Ada County, I had some interesting interview experiences. Here are a few:

- One man came to the sheriff's office for his interview. The interviewer asked, "Did you know you have an active warrant?" He responded, "Yes. Will that impact me getting the job?" It did. They arrested him.
- Another man came for his interview very mellow. Marijuana was illegal in Idaho at the time (still is as of this writing), so drug use questions are part of the interview process for sheriff's office deputies. They asked him if he had ever smoked marijuana. "Yes," he said. They followed up, "How recently have you smoked marijuana?" He responded, "Right before this interview in my car." I give him credit for the honesty. He, too, didn't get the job.
- On a résumé, someone once put, "Height/weight proportionate." That made me laugh, I don't know what that means! Equally tall as round?
- Ironically, an employee associated with the Drug Court program failed a drug test. The irony is only half of the story. This employee was fired, then applied for the job when it opened again. Hey, it's worth a shot!
- One lady told us upfront that she wanted to keep collecting unemployment instead of working

so she gave us instructions on how to let the unemployment office know that she applied for the job and wasn't selected rather than actually applying.

- Candidate on the phone inquiring about a work crew leader in our juvenile court services department: "Do you hire felons?" Our recruiter answered, "Depends on the felony." He asked, "What if it was lewd conduct with a minor?"

On the other hand, I'll be the first to admit that, as employers and organizations, we must set the right tone for the hiring and interviewing experiences. Unfortunately, we make some mistakes or have some poor practices ourselves. I've seen wild job announcements in my day. Here are a few:

- A job posting for a lifeguard that (I'm guessing accidentally) claimed to allow telecommuting
- For an executive assistant role: "Must be attractive; massages to help the boss relax [as he does mixed martial arts], willing to do cooking/ cleaning/prep work"
- Then there is this gem[1]:

> CONSTRUCTION WORKERS NEEDED: Lake Fork area. Please do not apply if you oversleep, have court often, do not have a babysitter every day, have to get rides to work later than our work day begins, experience flat tires every week, have to hold on to a cell phone all day, or will become an expert at your job with no need to learn or take advice after the first day. Must be able to talk and work at the same time. Must also remember to come back to work after lunch. Should not expect to receive gold stars for being on time. If you qualify, leave name and number at

Beyond poor job postings, we occasionally cancel or reschedule interviews, we might take a long time to get back to applicants or don't get back to them at all; we might be rude or dismissive, ask way too much of candidates, or set up an uncomfortable interview process. We need to do better.

While some hiring processes don't go well, I hope we have all had wonderful experiences where our businesses and work lives have drastically improved because we have made the right hire. Think about the person you hired who has made the biggest impact on you. If a name popped into your head, please send them a thank-you note. Go ahead, I'll wait…

What was their name, and what was it about them that made the biggest impact on you?

_____

I hope all of you reading this are contributing to your workplace in a way that makes people feel grateful that you were hired.

I like to say, "Start selection with reflection." We often need to pause to consider what we really need and the best way to structure our hiring process and decision-making structure so that we choose the best person. Please let me share with you a few tips that have helped my team to make the right hires more regularly, with a lot of credit to Jason Baker at Guidant as we learned and tested these strategies together.

Truly Define the Role

The best and first place to focus our reflection is understanding what we really want from a role. (See "Chapter 20: My Dream Job Description.") Here, I'll explain why. I've seen job announcements that require high levels of expertise in very different areas, such as search engine optimization (SEO), accounting, and recruiting. We'll save ourselves a lot of time chasing unicorns if we don't list such unrealistic requirements to start with. Conversely, if we're too vague about what we need or in such a dire need that we'll hire anybody, many will not be a good fit.

At the healthcare company I worked for, we often hired great people to be caregivers who quit within the first week because we were not clear that some of their responsibilities would be cooking or doing laundry. I think some hiring managers were waiting until the applicants came on board before telling them about the more challenging parts of the job, thinking they would stay. Many didn't. Being crystal clear about top priority needs for the role helped. We saw improved retention, especially in the first few weeks, when we shared with candidates all of the aspects of the job up front.

I learned in a call center setting that hiring only people who are bubbly and friendly, which seemed like the best strategy because they would be great to work with and would be the best with clients, didn't work as planned. We realized that while they were great co-workers, some additional refining of the role was needed because these very friendly folks often had a hard time telling people bad news, or took complaints personally, or spent too much time chatting with clients. We needed people who had those skills and understood those expectations, who could also engage in a friendly way. Lack of clarity created discomfort for people who were not at their very best in the role, and it wasn't fair that we put them in that position.

Assign a Candidate Experience Owner

We have a lot of recruiters and HR professionals who do a great job of hiring the right people in the short term. Zooming out and having a single person who owns the whole candidate experience will ensure that all applicants are treated fairly, respectfully, and positively. Top candidates will most likely accept the job, and those not selected will be more likely to engage in future opportunities and not leave poor reviews about their experience. I've had many experiences of top candidates accepting our offer over competing offers (even higher-paying ones) because of how they felt during our interview process. The candidate experience should be an extension of a great employee experience. I've also had the privilege of seeing great candidates who were not selected, or accepted a different offer at first, then engage with us when another opportunity arose and got selected. A great candidate experience creates an employer brand for long-term recruiting success. Having a clear owner increases the odds that this excellent and on-brand experience is delivered.

Publish the Hiring Range

I was on the fence about this for a long time. I saw benefits and trade-offs and opted to leave the wage for discussion after the fact, despite always having a predetermined range. Since testing this, I have been so impressed by the benefits to both the candidates and our team that I truly wish I had done this much sooner. The candidates have clarity upfront on whether they want to apply and self-select in or out based on this hiring range, which creates an easier process for recruiters and hiring managers to focus on just those who already accept the posted range. For one role, we often got two thousand applications, many that were looking for pay higher than our pay range. By publishing the wage, this was cut by 40 percent. We still had amazing candidates and hundreds of other candidates spent their time on roles that were within their desired wage range instead of spending time on our process for a role that wasn't a good fit. Win-win. Start selection with reflection by establishing and publishing the hiring range. Many states in the U.S. are passing pay transparency laws. If you're not doing this yet, we may all likely be required to in the future. Let's embrace it now.

Simple Application Process

We often overcomplicate our lives. I've found that simplifying our hiring process generates the best results. Here are some ideas on how to do this:

- Kill cover letter requirements. (See "Chapter 27: Traditional HR vs. HR Evolutions" for an in-depth explanation.)
- Reduce the number of questions asked on the application. In my experience, a maximum of three works best.
- Allow people to submit résumés electronically, and let's never require someone who has done this to also fill in their information in another place. It's frustrating and damaging our candidate experience reputations.

Interview Questions and Process

I often get asked what the best interview questions are. I really believe that there isn't a single great question, and it's better for people to use any personal favorites that work for them. The best practice for a fruitful discussion is to have a combination of multiple good questions and to set the right tone in the meeting. I'll share a few of my favorite questions, along with some additional tips, to consider during interviews:

- Favorite question #1: What questions do you have for us?
  - I believe so strongly that each candidate will be making such a large life decision to join our company that an interview should be just as much about them interviewing us as it is about us interviewing them. Make adequate time at the end of each interview for all their questions to be answered so they can make an informed decision.
- Favorite question #2: Tell me about a professional failure you had, or mistake you made, and what you learned from it.
  - Notice this is not a general question about weaknesses but rather a request for a specific example to see if they have the self-awareness to recognize this in their life, the humility and honesty to share something with us, and the resilience and desire to grow.
- Favorite question #3: What are you most excited about learning and experiencing in this role?
  - I'll finish the chapter with how important this question was for me personally. I think this allows people the freedom to envision their best self in the role and imagine how they want to grow. This is important because I want to make sure I know what

their ambitions are so we can commit to delivering on those, or being honest if it reveals that we aren't a good fit.

- Favorite question #4: Please select one of our company values, and give us an example of how you recently demonstrated this value at work.
- Provide candidates with questions in advance.
  - I'm amazed at how often I hear people say, "They have good experience, but they didn't interview well." So what? Are we paying them to be professional interviewees? I also hear interviewers who love to try to catch interviewees "off-guard" or see them "think on their feet." Why? Is that part of the job they'll be doing? If it is, then I get it. If it's not, let's do our part to make these interviews more pleasant and interesting.
  - We want to make the best hire possible. To do that, we genuinely want the best answers to our well-thought-out questions. To get those answers, let's help candidates feel MORE comfortable, not less. One of the best ways is to provide the questions in advance. Now they can provide excellent answers without the pressure of thinking on the spot, which many people just don't do well.
- Have a designated note-taker.
  - Have you ever been in an interview where one person asks a question and, as you're answering the question, you're talking to the tops of everyone's heads as they look down to scribble notes? I like interviews to feel like conversations, not interrogations. I usually designate one person to ask all the questions and one to be the note-taker; all

others can take notes and ask follow-up questions if needed. I share all this with the candidate at the beginning of the interview so they know the reason for this approach. I've had many people tell me they really appreciate this style of interview because they always had someone making eye contact with them, so it felt like they were having a genuine conversation.

Include Culture Champions

Talent recognizes talent. Use successful culture champions in the organization in the hiring process. This provides three important benefits:

- This further engages and celebrates current culture champions.
- Culture champions will recognize others like them who will thrive in the organization based on core values.
- Candidates can feel more comfortable asking them questions about what it's "really" like to work there and get honest answers from people in roles similar to what they're interviewing for.

Measure for Continuous Improvement

We must get faster at hiring great talent. Measuring end results and process times will help us identify areas to improve. While the actual targets will vary by industry and company, my favorite end-result measurements for hiring are the following:

- **Time-to-hire** (from the time a hiring manager notifies us of an open role until the role is closed with an accepted offer). In general, under forty-two days is a good target. For urgent roles and/or in times of high competition, this may need to be faster.
- **Vacancy rate** (the number of roles open divided by the total number of positions in the organization). I target 5 percent or less. Any higher than this and it usually starts to put additional pressure and stress on remaining team members, which can accelerate additional turnover.
- **First-year retention**. This is a quality metric to make sure that we hire and keep top talent as we get faster at making hiring decisions.

When Jason Baker led our recruiting team to define and document our hiring process in a simple flowchart, this allowed us to select different portions to measure. Here are a couple of metrics we tested that made a surprising impact on our hiring process as we made improvements to these time frames:

- **Time from notice to job posting**. We didn't realize how many days passed before we were notified of needing to post a job, either because someone submitted their resignation, there was a promotion, or a new approved head count. We also noticed that even when we got the notice, several steps still had to be taken before we were ready to post. By working to get notifications sooner and then doing more prep work (job descriptions, interview questions, candidate scorecard) ahead of time, we improved this time from over seven days to two or less. That makes a huge difference in speed.

- **Time from separation to start date of the new hire**. This was used to measure the time that the team was without a team member. We want to minimize this so one turnover doesn't lead to multiple. We tried to see if we could extend people's resignation periods, posting jobs as soon as possible, and starting new hires as soon as they can begin.

Use a Scorecard

It can be hard to compare candidates, and especially to remember them all clearly, when many interviews are conducted within a short period. Biases also tend to work their way in. Using an objective scorecard that has a combination of key competencies, company values, and any specific team values can help. One might look like this:

Candidate Scorecard	Key competencies & values	Rating: 1 (Low) – 5 (High)	Rating notes
Key competency 1	Supervisor skills		
Key competency 2	Client escalation management		
Key competency 3	Budgeting		
Company value 1	Compassion		

Company value 2	Excellence		
Company value 3	Trust		
Team value 1	Innovation		
Team value 2	Flexibility		
	TOTAL		

Make time after each interview to rate the candidate from 1 to 5 in each category. Rank candidates as you go.

Reference Checks

See "Chapter 27: Traditional HR vs. HR Evolutions" for my thoughts on reference checks.

Conclusion

As I was heading into my last semester for my HR management bachelor's degree at Boise State University, I wanted to get an internship to start getting experience and expand my network. I was fortunate to receive two offers for paid internships. One was at Washington Group International (WGI), which was later purchased by URS Corporation; one was with Ada County's Human Resources department. Ada County is Idaho's largest county and had about sixteen hundred employees at the time. Despite WGI offering me 50 percent more pay at a time when money was very important (newly married, student loans, etc.), I chose Ada County.

It came down to one question that Ada County interviewers—the amazing Cassie Danell and Kim Osborn—asked that WGI did not: "What do you want to learn and experience in your internship?" I could tell they really meant that. I trusted that we would be able to customize an experience that would be most meaningful for me and that I would be able to contribute in ways best aligned with my skills and interests. Fortunately, after graduation several months later, Ada County created a full-time position for me where I stayed for over five years because they were truly committed to my growth and were an amazing team to work with.

I am grateful for every company and hiring manager that took a chance on me. They recognized me as a seed worth growing. By treating all candidates with respect, simplifying where possible, measuring our success, and opening our minds to different approaches, we will find the best people to invest in long-term who will be the best fit. That is how we can "start selection with reflection."

On a personal level, I hope this helps you or a loved one avoid the disappointment of not seeing a barbecue sunflower seed fail to grow into a beautiful barbecue sunflower plant.

Visit HRYouKiddingMe.com for sample hiring-for-culture templates.

Hiring for Culture 2—The Selection Spectrum

I was once in a difficult situation hiring for a role. My top candidate was able to start in three weeks, and another candidate could start right away. Because I was putting pressure on myself to get the role filled to get immediate help, I hired the second candidate. They were not a great fit, primarily for my leadership style. They called me a micromanager when I explained that the monthly newsletter they would be creating for six hundred employees would be reviewed by another person before being sent out. That individual only lasted a few months before finding a great job outside of our organization.

Have you been there? Or maybe you've looked up and realized that the only people on one manager's team are people from their alma mater or book club? Or it takes a long time to fill a role because the hiring manager is looking for that "perfect candidate"?

Enter the Selection Spectrum.

On our own, unstructured decisions may be influenced by our biases, pressures, experiences, and timing. This usually leads to poor hiring decisions. When it comes to hiring, poor decisions can be very costly. Costs of a poor hire, according to Gallup, is half to double the employee's annual pay.[1] Negative impact is high when also factoring in the damage this can do to client relationships, team productivity, culture, and the time and energy needed to work with and exit a poor hire.[2] Only to be back again hiring.

Selection Spectrum

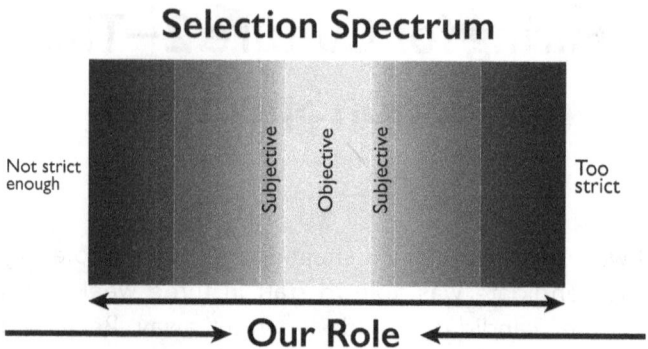

Not strict enough — Subjective — Objective — Subjective — Too strict

Our Role

Our role is to push decision-making into the center zone where there is mostly objectivity, with some allowable degree of subjectivity. This will give us the best chance of making a good long-term hire.

On one side of the Selection Spectrum is the tendency to not be strict enough in our decision-making. The chart below lists the various reasons we might not be investing enough thought into our decision. It's important to evaluate our process before and during to see if we notice any of these problems, then work to adjust the process to push our decision into the safest place in the middle. The halo effect is taking a single positive characteristic and allowing that to minimize negative traits and/or increase the positive judgments on other unrelated factors.[3]

Selection Spectrum

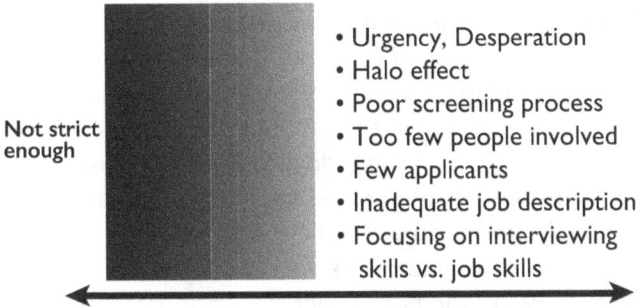

Not strict enough

- Urgency, Desperation
- Halo effect
- Poor screening process
- Too few people involved
- Few applicants
- Inadequate job description
- Focusing on interviewing skills vs. job skills

On the other side, we might tend to be too strict in our hiring decisions. Not bringing someone on board quickly can drain existing team members and may cause additional burnout and separations. The reasons for this can vary, as shown below.

Selection Spectrum

- Unconscious Bias
- Horn effect
- Seeking complete consensus
- Too many people involved
- Searching for "perfect" candidate

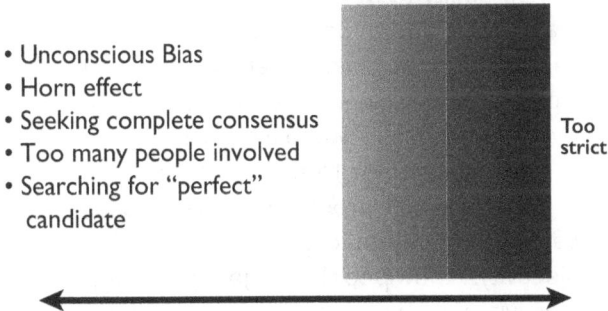

Too strict

I've seen this manifest itself in a variety of ways, always with the end result of losing out on great talent. Sometimes candidates accept other jobs because it takes so long to schedule too many interviewers for too many rounds of interviews. I've seen situations where the decision-maker isn't clear, so too many people are trying to get to a complete consensus. I've seen jobs that require a master's degree that pay twelve dollars per hour. I almost didn't get a job as a teller at U.S. Bank because the hiring manager told the all-female teller staff at the time that she didn't really want to hire a man.

I've seen people not be interviewed because of a misspelled word on a résumé or not get hired because they were one minute late to an interview. That can be an example of the horn effect, the opposite of the halo effect. Being very strict on spelling or punctuality might be a good practice for some roles, unless it takes twice as long to fill a role and that extra time is draining other resources. Then we've probably wandered right into the "too strict" category.

One step I've taken to avoid falling into the "too strict" trap is to stop asking about gaps in employment. I've seen no correlation between a gap in employment and their ability to do a job if we select them. Rather, I see a massive and undeserved overemphasis by some organizations that makes them miss out on talented people. Let's make sure we're asking the right questions of everyone to ensure we're a good fit for each other.

Again, our goal is to make a good hiring decision and to push our processes, ourselves, and others toward a primarily objective decision with acceptable subjectivity. I know people are going to struggle with the subjectivity part because unconscious bias can impact decisions here.

Selection Spectrum

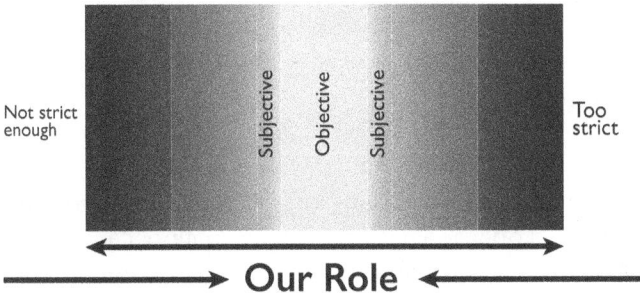

Our Role

I do not believe it is possible to remove all subjectivity from a hiring decision. So I think we must embrace it with some of the guardrails mentioned on both sides of the Selection Spectrum. Here are a couple of examples.

First, we might be blessed to have amazing candidates who all meet the objective criteria. They have the right experience, are within the salary range, and check all the job requirements. How can we decide? There are appropriate subjective factors like culture fit or culture add, the external network they might bring, their attitudes, or how well they will get along with team members, leaders, or clients.

A positive personal example of a culture add is when I got hired at Guidant Financial. Even though my experience and education met all the requirements, I still had many different interviews before getting offered the role. The objective part was easy, and there were probably many other candidates who checked the boxes. David Nilssen, co-founder and CEO at the time, told me it was important to him that they hired someone they could trust to be a culture steward who would balance out a hard-charging leadership team. They had a lot of energy and ideas and needed help from someone who was organized and experienced to prioritize and channel that energy into well-executed projects. It took great discipline to create a hiring process tailored for this role so they could make both an objective and subjective decision that they believed would serve them best.

Before you hire your next role, look at your hiring plan. Is it too strict or not strict enough? Is there a clear decision-maker, too many or too few interviewers or rounds? Look again as you're evaluating candidates. Do you feel like you're outside the safe zone? If so, in what direction and how can you work back to the middle? (See the previous chapter for ideas like using a scorecard to help.)

While this is not perfect, I hope this helps prevent the pain of hiring the wrong person or waiting too long to get someone on board. Instead, you find the right person at the right time.

4

Good Onboarding is the Best Recruiting Insurance

Write down the three strongest emotions you felt when you started your last job. Or, if it's been a while, imagine you are going to start a new job. What are the three most powerful emotions you feel?

1.
2.
3.

Let's hang onto those for a minute.

According to data from the Society for Human Resource Management released in 2022, the average cost per hire is $4,683.[1] According to the United States Bureau of Labor Statistics, 77.2 million people were hired in 2022.[2] The quick math there estimates the cost of annual hiring in the United States alone to be over $361 billion. My guess is, if we have something worth over $361 billion, we will want to protect and insure that investment. After all, the insurance company Lloyds of London is reported to have insured David Beckham's legs, Bruce Springsteen's voice, and Troy Polamalu's hair.[3]

Now that I've somehow managed to talk about David Beckham's legs, let's talk about leverage.

Leverage is the exertion of force with a lever—i.e., to use something to maximum advantage. Building the pyramids, launching rockets into space, and even golf swings expertly use leverage as a method to invest action for maximum results. An important principle is that there are high leverage points in our work where effort returns the greatest value. I've become fascinated by leverage: where can I apply my limited time and energy to receive the biggest gain?

With infinite work to do, we must prioritize where our efforts and skills will have the highest leverage. In the employee life cycle, I believe their onboarding experience is the highest leverage point to invest in. Good onboarding is the best recruiting insurance. Small efforts here achieve maximum results. Why? Let's go back to the beginning of the chapter and the emotions you feel or felt when starting a new job. Often, when people are honest, they will use words like *scared*, *nervous*, *anxious*, *uncertain*, or *embarrassed*. When the potential for strong emotions is high, our opportunity for positive impact is equally high.

First impressions matter.

I like a comment the University of Melbourne made after researching this phenomenon: "First impressions are instantly made but, ironically, they can stubbornly last a lifetime."[4] Committing to a positive first impression during onboarding, a high-leverage moment, can create a positive foundation for each team member that will hopefully last a lifetime.

Here are a few ideas that have worked for me:

- **Hire in cohorts**. If this is possible, starting with and having regular interactions with other new hires creates a powerful connection among the cohort.
- **Assign a buddy**. At Guidant, we call this our "Partner in Crime" program. It's amazing how many questions we have when we're new that we're too embarrassed to ask. When is payday? Are those two married? When did the company start? Why do we do things this way? A few casual meetings in the beginning with a buddy or partner-in-crime can be the perfect safe place to ask questions and make a new friend right away.
- **Office space and technology equipment are available and configured**. Too many first days get off to a rough start when space and technology aren't ready. I've learned that time with our technology team as the new hires' very first step creates the best foundation for them to be confident the rest of the day. A friendly technology person as one of their very first contacts on the first day dramatically changes the onboarding experience. When I worked in an office, I liked to send a picture to a new hire a few days before their first day showing them their own space, nameplate, and laptop to let them know that we were ready and excited for them to join the team.
- **Create a very organized first day and first week**. Communicate this to them before they start. Knowing where to go, when, who to talk to, and the expectations for those beginning moments are simple yet powerful.

- **See "Chapter 6: Culture Is Connection"** to use the framework there specifically for onboarding and learning how to intentionally connect each new team member to purpose, leaders, and each another. We try to hire everyone on Mondays. That way, on their first day, we can introduce them in our weekly company meeting. We also discuss our values and principles, and I send them a personal welcome note.
- **Allow some time for self-discovery**. Give new hires a chance to set up their office, walk around the building, check out the website, personalize their computer settings, and explore the systems and programs they'll be using. Use cautiously and intentionally, though; otherwise, this may feel like abandonment.
- **Welcome gifts are a great touch**. This can be company-branded items, treats, or a plant. We like to ask new team members what their favorite candy or snacks are, and send them some.
- **We've tested and seen success with a scavenger hunt-type of checklist for new hires to manage as they have downtime**. Important videos to watch, practicing getting information from our employee resource center, and publicly recognizing another team member are part of the hunt for them to earn some branded items.
- **Ask for feedback**. We send brief surveys at thirty days and ninety days. We want to know right away what is working and what is not.

I try to personally send a message to every team member before they start. I also send a welcome message to every team member on their first day. The first day for a new team member is important enough for me to invest time to ensure they feel welcome.

One of my favorite messages, which I send to every new team member sometime in their first week, is telling them to give themselves a break. Awesome people normally think they need to be impressive and make a difference on Day One or Week One or Month One. I invite them to relax, be patient with themselves, and try to have fun instead of putting pressure on themselves. I've received some very touching responses from people after I've shared that with them.

A few years ago, our neighbor's wood fence was in shambles. They spent a lot of time, money, and energy putting in a new wood fence. Then they didn't paint or stain it to protect it. After just a couple of years, it was looking weathered and worn all over again. This neutralized all the hard work of putting in the new fence in the first place. They didn't protect their time, energy, and cost investment.

We're busy. We work hard to hire the best talent we can. New team members are nervous. This is a high-leverage moment. They deserve the best onboarding experience for making a major life decision to join our team and they will remember it. We need to preserve the talent we've hired, and good onboarding is our best chance.

Offboarding Is the New Onboarding

Over the years, I've accumulated some funny stories, news articles, and pictures. I have two pictures that still make me laugh every time I see them. The first picture is a job advertisement from a newspaper for a local hospital system. Featuring a smiling nurse, the ad says, "St. Luke's Nampa Medical is now firing for the following positions…," going on to list about eight positions that they are "firing" for.[1] I'm guessing a lot of people in the roles on that list were pretty nervous.

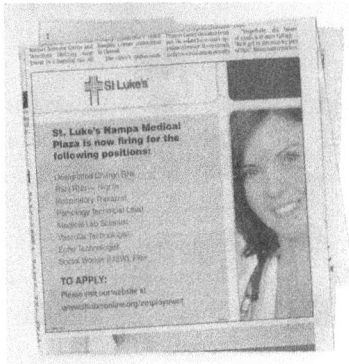

The second picture is from when I worked at Ada County, during a time when our department was relocating within the courthouse. Our new space was being constructed from a previously open area, so our building maintenance team was adding walls, plumbing, rooms, doors, and so on. This included a file room for locked employee files. In a hilarious and unfortunate Freudian slip, when they were making the placards for all the new rooms, the one they created and hung said FIRE ROOM instead of FILE ROOM. That was totally serious and not a joke. I sure hope all of us Human Resources professionals are helping the world see that we add value in many areas outside of "firing people."

As you can probably guess, I don't love the word *firing*. There continues to be a lot in the news about workplace trends, from quiet quitting to massive social media blowups and how organizations are both responding to these behaviors and initiating their own exits—layoffs, company-wide memos, and ultimatums about returning to the office from remote working. You may have heard about the auto repair shop that paid a final paycheck to an exiting employee with over ninety thousand oily pennies dumped on his driveway.[2]

How people exit the organization is just as important as how they enter it. Let me share some of my favorite messages I've recently received. Each of these was from an individual who left the organization, then wanted to come back.

- "After twelve months, I realize I REALLY miss the culture and people at Guidant. I was wondering if there is a possible way I could return?"
- "To say I miss Guidant would be an understatement! I am writing to inquire about the possibility of returning."
- "I hope that Guidant is thriving and that all is well with you. I'm enjoying good health, and while it's been a blessing to be able to take some time for my family and self, I would be interested in exploring a return to Guidant."

Once a great culture has been established, it's important to maintain it. One area that I find a tremendous amount of value (and one that I feel many organizations and Human Resources professionals overlook) is a great offboarding mentality and process.

When great people leave the organization, it's natural to have a range of emotions—guilt, frustration, fear, embarrassment, betrayal, and other strong feelings. To be honest, I still have a hard time not taking it personally, especially if it's someone on my team. My natural response is to freeze in a state of denial for longer than I should before acting. I have to make conscious shifts in my mindset to create better actions. If we don't do this, we can end up creating an experience for exiting employees that leaves a bad taste in their mouths—they feel ignored, rushed out of the company, underappreciated, disrespected, or other negative emotions.

I like to say, "Offboarding is the new onboarding." Onboarding gets a lot of attention, and it should. It is a key high-leverage point in time when our investments in people can pay the greatest dividends. (See "Chapter 4: Good Onboarding Is the Best Recruiting Insurance.") Similarly, I believe offboarding creates a high-leverage point where investing, even with simple actions in exiting team members can leave them feeling positive about their experience and contributions.

There are many benefits for an organization when people leave positively:

1. **Boomerang employees**. Great team members may return! The Corporate Culture and Boomerang Employee Study by Workplace Trends gave the following data:
   a. Fifteen percent of employees have boomeranged back to a former employer.
   b. Forty percent of employees say they would consider boomeranging back to a company.[3]

   The benefits of boomerang employees are significant: less recruiting time, values alignment, more immediate impact, excitement from them and other team members being reunited, understanding the company processes, policies, and systems, and many others.[4]

2. **Employee referrals**. When I joined Guidant Financial in 2019, Nick, our recruiter, gave his two-week notice on my first day. He had been with the company for a few months and received

a great offer to return to the company he had worked at before, in an industry he was passionate about. After he left, we kept in touch. I was happy he was in a place that was fulfilling for him. We kept checking in occasionally on our work and personal lives and getting perspectives on different challenges and opportunities. When he left, we were able to promote someone from within the company until she got enough experience to get hired by Facebook. This was an awesome career step for her. Back to looking for a new recruiter, Nick put me in touch with Jason Baker, someone he had met and highly recommended. We interviewed Jason, hired him, and he has been adding tremendous value at Guidant for over three years now, helping us transform our recruiting and onboarding practice to fully remote, then helping us nearly triple our headcount, hiring hundreds of people during that time.

3. **Client referrals**. For my last two companies, one in healthcare and the other in finance, I've seen former employees come back to use our services themselves and refer others to partner with us.

4. **Positive reviews**. People often take the opportunity to leave company reviews on different websites. People leaving the organization positively, even if they had some challenges, are more likely to include positive aspects of the job instead of using it as an opportunity to only showcase negative aspects. A respectful exit may even prevent someone from leaving a negative review.

5. **Living core values of the company**. I once had someone tell me about their experience when they were leaving an organization. They said this was a company known to treat employees great… "until you leave, then they treat you horribly." By different people, she felt ignored and pressured to stay. Some tried to make her feel guilty and ungrateful. I suspect most companies have core values that encourage team members to treat each other in respectful ways, even if those adjectives or behaviors vary slightly. Team members who are leaving the organization for any reason create an opportunity for us to truly demonstrate those core values. After all, this is when those values mean the most because this is a situation when it may be the hardest to adhere to them.

Here are some tips for creating a great offboarding experience. In addition to the normal administration of any separation from the organization, these are the ABCDs of an exceptional offboarding experience:

- **Announce.** Notify people of the change. At smaller companies, this can be the whole company; for larger companies, notifying those most impacted by the change is sufficient. Be sure to consult the person leaving on the timing and method for announcing the separation since they may want to tell certain people first before the whole company finds out. At Guidant, we use our Monday Morning Stand-up, a weekly all-company meeting, to announce who is joining the organization, who is being promoted, and who is leaving the organization—

regardless of their reason for leaving. Visibility trumps mystery. Every time.

- **Balance.** Often, when someone is exiting the organization, we swing the pendulum of activity too far in either direction. Some might uninvite them to all meetings and stop seeking their feedback, leaving them feeling isolated and ignored. Or, in a rush to extract every bit of productivity and knowledge from them, we overwhelm them with more meetings and/or time-consuming tasks like "document everything you do and how you do it." Let's balance this by engaging with them on what's reasonable to expect during their notice period. Let's help them feel like they've added value during their remaining time with the organization without unnecessary stress, isolation, or confusion. If the company is terminating an employee, this is a good opportunity to consider paying them out for a short period. I prefer for terminations to happen in the morning so we can pay them for the rest of the day at least, the rest of the week if possible.

- **Celebrate.** During the weekly announcement of people exiting, we thank them for their contributions and share their excitement for the next career journey, and we encourage everyone in the company to reach out to thank them now before they officially transition and to stay in touch with them afterward.

- **Discover.** Even though critics will say that exit interviews are "too late" because we should be doing stay interviews all along, there is still important information to collect from team members who are leaving the organization.

In addition, this sends the message to team members that their perspective matters and we're making time to learn about what's exciting for them about their next opportunity, when and why they started looking for another role, if there's anything that would have kept them at the organization, and other responses that could help us continually improve the employee experience. While I'm a fan of stay interviews during any team member's tenure, I've found a special kind of honesty and perspective when doing exit interviews that is refreshing and helpful. These conversations also create opportunities to celebrate their contributions and express appreciation for them, which lasts long after they have left.

The ABCDs are all actions to take with anyone leaving the organization and can be done in any order. If we want to add an "E" to our ABCDs, it could be "Engage." Once someone has left the organization, there are some fun ways to continue to engage with former teammates.

First, I like to help people adopt an "alumni" mindset. Much like universities, alumni groups can be powerful groups of people with great knowledge, experience, and other contacts in their networks. Calling them alumni and treating them as such, like graduates from our organization, is one way to positively recognize their growth beyond our organization and sets the stage for making time for other efforts to engage this group.

Next, at Guidant we have an appointed "Commissioner of Fun." His name is Paul Cook, and he loves combining three of his favorite things: connection, sports, and competition. He is the champion of our annual March Madness experience, our NFL pick-ems competition, and our Super Bowl pool. Paul has deliberately included prior participants, even if they have since moved on from the organization. This has created continuing bonds of friendship among current team members and alumni.

Also, every month I set a reminder on my calendar with my other monthly commitments to reach out to Guidant alumni. Often, we're already connected on LinkedIn. I try to connect with all current and prior team members there so I can be involved in their achievements. Other times, I'll track down personal emails. Either way, I usually reach out to five to eight people to check in on their new job, to ask for feedback on a question I have, to congratulate them on new successes, or just to say hello. Here is a quote from an alumnus I reached out to who later that day emailed our recruiter:

"I received an email from Cory just checking on me and that got to me! To get an email like that really shows what a great group of people Guidant has! I have missed that! I write in hopes of having the opportunity of coming back to Guidant! If this can be a possibility, please let me know!"

In the last year, Guidant has had four people return to the company, and we have another four individuals who have expressed interest in returning when the right role is open again for them. While there are many factors, I sincerely believe that creating a positive offboarding experience is a high leverage point in time when people will distinctly remember, good or bad, how they felt during that transition.

So I'll restate this: How people exit the organization is just as important as how they enter it, to them and the company.

SECTION 2

Transforming Culture

6

Culture Is Connection

My son Phoenix is an awesome soccer player now. I say "now" because he's come a long way. When he first played soccer as a four-year-old, his strategy was to take a wide stance and plant himself in the middle of the field. Then never move. He would smile and enjoy looking all around him watching everyone else play the game while he rooted himself spread-legged into the field. Occasionally, the ball would touch his foot, and he would just look up excitedly waiting for someone else to kick it. I have pictures from multiple games to prove that this was a season-long strategy.

Even though he had fun, the game happened all around him—people ran, kicked, scored goals, and blocked goals. He didn't make any intentional contributions or attempt to shape the game. He let the game come to him and define itself.

Many of us feel this way about our workplace culture. In my work through Cornell, and as a consultant, I'll often ask questions about how people have defined important workplace elements such as culture or talent strategy. Surprisingly, many say that they haven't ever defined it. Just like my son's soccer game, the game of culture is happening all around us, whether we choose to define it or not. If we want to take a more active role in playing this game, we must be intentional and have a plan. Otherwise, the game will be defined by others.

Based on my experience of successfully transitioning a company with two main U.S. hubs (Bellevue, Washington, and Boise, Idaho) into a fully and permanently remote organization with over two hundred team members in fourteen states and three countries while recently winning a #1 Best Places to Work in Idaho award, I can summarize what I've learned very simply: Culture is connection.[1]

Culture Is Connection

There are a lot of different ways to define culture. Most are accurate and are associated with a common set of values. The problem I have is that these definitions are hard to measure and act on. Culture can be a powerful differentiator and competitive advantage, so in this chapter, I'll show you how to measure culture and take practical steps toward building and maintaining it through connection.

"Connection," in this context, refers to three work elements: purpose, leaders, and each other.

Purpose	Team members must be connected to the purpose of the organization. This includes the reason that the organization exists, the positive impact we're trying to make in the world, our customers, and the future direction of the organization. Being clear about this message, and finding special ways to connect individuals to how they help achieve the purpose, is a critical alignment for an impactful culture.

Leaders	Each team member must feel connected to those leading the company. The most important relationship is that person's direct supervisor. Each person must also trust senior leaders of the organization and be aligned with the company values and principles set by those leaders.
Each Other	Even though each person will need or want a different level of connection in the workplace, having strong relationships with co-workers and opportunities to get to know each other is critical.

If you're a Venn Diagram person, here you go:

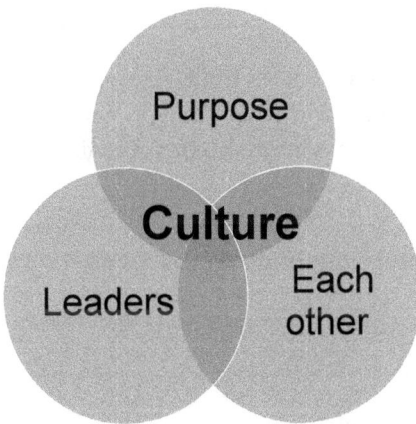

Along with these three core elements of connection and culture, an additional factor is people's personal preferences. Each individual will be different in their wants and needs around workplace connection. The best way to address this is by providing a menu of opportunities, some required and some optional, that will create these connections. Everyone will receive the same opportunities, while empowering each team member to customize their connection experiences.

Culture Is Connection Framework

Let's try this on, and see how it fits. Take a few minutes to consider different activities or elements of your company culture and see where they fit into this framework. If something fits in multiple categories equally (purpose, leaders, each other), add it to each. Otherwise, try to define where it creates the greatest connection.

Culture Is Connection Framework	Connection to Purpose	Connection to Leaders	Connection to Each Other
Required			
Optional			

How does your current framework look? Where are you strong, and what can you celebrate? Are there areas where there might be opportunities to strengthen connection?

Here is how Guidant looked before we understood the power of this framework and before we went fully remote:

Culture Is Connection Framework	Connection to Purpose	Connection to Leaders	Connection to Each Other
Required	Monday Morning Stand-up	People Celebrations Regular supervisor 1:1	Monthly team building Regular team meetings
Optional	Client Testimonials Swag		Monthly people newsletter Microsoft Teams Channel: Cheers! Committees: Connection

As we went fully remote, we recognized that we needed to be much more intentional in creating connection opportunities. We added a few additional items (bolded) to create this framework:

Culture Is Connection Framework	Connection to Purpose	Connection to Leaders	Connection to Each Other
Required	Monday Morning Stand-up **Remote Code of Conduct** **Quarterly Engagement Survey**	People Celebrations Regular supervisor 1:1	Monthly teambuilding Regular team meetings **Annual all-day event** **Pictures in Microsoft Teams**
Optional	Client Testimonials Swag **Employee Resource Center**	**Leadership Coffee** **Weekly CEO Email**	Monthly people newsletter Microsoft Teams Channel: Cheers! and **Breakroom** Committees: Connection **Diversity, Equity, & Inclusion (DEI)**

Please see the Appendix for a description of each activity. You'll likely notice that many of these activities will create connections in multiple areas, so I've placed them in the area where they make the greatest connection.

In case it's helpful to see how this plays out throughout the year:

Cadence	Connection Opportunity
Weekly	Monday Morning Stand-up, CEO email
Monthly	Team meeting, Supervisor 1:1, Connection committee event, team building
Quarterly	Leadership coffee, engagement survey, DEI Committee discussion
Semi-Annual	People Celebration
Annual	Guidant Connection Event, Swag
Ongoing	Remote Code of Conduct, Employee Resource Center, Client Testimonials, Microsoft Teams Channels: Breakroom and Cheers! Personal pictures in Teams

How to Measure

We've now seen how we can take actionable steps toward building culture through connection. Now let's use data to measure our current state and progress. The simplest way is asking team members directly how connected they feel to each of the three areas: purpose, leaders, and each other. Then you can evaluate each area individually and combine them for a single connection score.

You can make variations of these questions to fit your organization or preference. At Guidant, because we believe the direct supervisor is the most important work relationship, we ask, "How supported do you feel by your direct supervisor?" There may be better questions we could ask to gauge how connected people feel to leaders. That's where we started, and the trend data is now too valuable (and useful enough as is) to make a change now.

Whatever you decide works best for you, stick with it over multiple survey cycles to celebrate the progress and course correct where needed. Here is how Guidant's employee connection scores have evolved over time. The high-water mark of 4.7 in September 2022 was right after our first annual remote Guidant Connection Event—taking a full day off to connect. That was a huge hit.

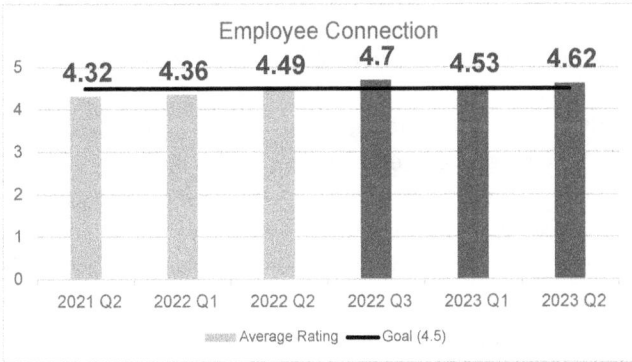

For those who love data and graphs, here's one more for you below. As an additional way to track connection and effectiveness through surveys, we asked the team what they found most meaningful. This graph helped us decide where to focus and where to evolve.

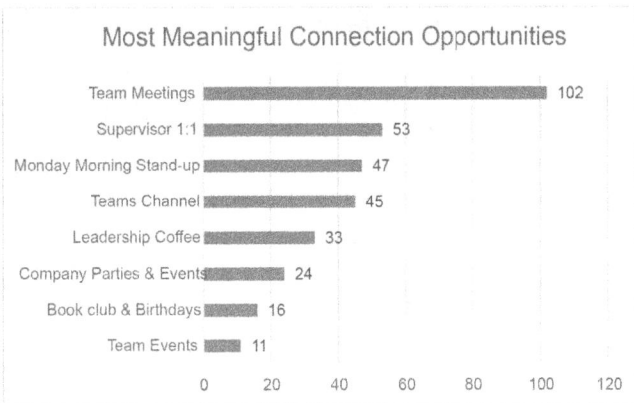

This will likely look very different for your organization, which is part of what makes this so enjoyable. Following the framework and measuring regularly can help all our organizations create more connection to our purpose, leaders, and each other. This connection will help us build and sustain a culture that will attract and retain the right people, driving our business forward and making positive impacts on our clients and communities.

Here are some of my favorite comments received from team members after applying this framework:

- "For a remote work environment, it doesn't get more engaged than this."
- "Guidant allows me to feel connected to both work and home, allowing me to maintain a work-life balance."
- "I'm more engaged than I've been on jobs where we all worked in an office together."

At the end of an all-day connection event that we held virtually, one of our longest-tenured team members (over seventeen years) asked if he could say something. We gave him space. He proceeded to tell the whole company that he has long been the biggest skeptic that people can be connected and successful remotely. That day made him a believer. He felt connected and energized. That person was Paul Cook, our amazing Commissioner of Fun.

If these are the results and responses you would like to see on your team or in your organization, be intentional about connection. The game of culture is happening all around us. As with soccer, we can watch it unfold as a spectator or get in there and score some goals. Go score some goals.

Remember, culture is connection.

Infusing Core Values Through the Whole Organization

When my wife and I bought our first house, I was looking forward to having an amazing yard. I always admired well-manicured landscaping and lush green lawns. The first year was great because we had new sod and a sprinkler system installed by experts. The second year was a different story: I began to get dry patches and different types of nasty weeds started infiltrating our yard. Grass didn't grow in places I wanted it to, and grew great in places I didn't want it to, like into our flower beds.

I got serious about it and went to work. I waged a war on those weeds. These clovers, dandelions, and morning glories didn't stand a chance. I spread pre-emergent granules plus a pellet-type of weed killer. I used a lawn-safe weed killer spray every day to keep the weeds out. I bought an awesome sprayer to strap on my back and felt like a Ghostbuster. Mostly because it is the nature of weeds to do so, and partly because we had a neighbor who seemed to be growing an intentional yard full of dandelions, it took a lot of effort that year to keep up with all the weeds.

At one point, we considered giving in and just having a clover lawn–popular in some places. Chemical-free and money-free options were available to me based on my research–digging them out one by one or placing a clear drinking glass on top of them to have the sun burn them. The result of all my efforts (and I have embarrassing pictures to prove it) was a brown lawn covered in weeds in varying degrees of health, depending upon how recently I had sprayed them. I had focused all my energy on the weeds.

It turns out that the best way to keep out unwanted weeds is to prevent them in the first place. I was asking the wrong question of people and the internet. I was asking "What is the best way to kill weeds" when I should have been asking, "What is the best way to prevent weeds from growing?" I spent a lot of time and energy researching and applying what I learned on the first question instead of seeking a better question and answer.

The best way to prevent weeds is to grow strong grass. Strong grass naturally keeps out weeds because there is less room for weeds to grow when the grass is healthy and thick.

The third year in our home we had amazingly green grass, despite our adjacent neighbors continuing their dandelion sanctuary in their yard next door. This time, we focused on growing green grass. I spent time calibrating our sprinklers. I learned the best time and the best amounts to water the lawn. I spent my time and money on fertilizer. I mulched my lawn to keep the good grass continually nourishing itself. I still killed a few weeds that popped up, although they became fewer and fewer. In the end, I had a beautiful lawn and spent half the money and half the time and energy when I focused on growing green grass instead of killing the weeds.

This story can be a powerful reminder of how we approach culture and people in our organization. If we spend all our time and energy on the weeds, the grass will not grow. In "Chapter 6: Culture Is Connection," I noted that a key element of culture is connection to leaders. While the direct supervisor is the most important work relationship, senior leaders play a critical role in defining, living, and recognizing core values. A positive culture, corporate effectiveness and growth, and happy customers become the green grass results of focusing on core values.

A few years ago, I became really fascinated by and curious about core values in organizations. I compared the values of the ten largest U.S. companies based on market capitalization. Even though Tesla was in the top ten, I excluded them because they didn't have publicly shared values that I could find. At the time, the other companies were the following, starting from the largest: Apple, Amazon, Microsoft, Google, Facebook, Berkshire Hathaway, Visa, Walmart, and Johnson & Johnson.

I found some interesting similarities between these nine very successful companies. First, the average number of values was five. This is a good benchmark. Personally, I think three to five is the sweet spot. Fewer than three leaves values being lived in the organization that are not represented and more than five can become difficult to remember and may conflict with one another.

I created a word cloud of the core values of these companies:

innovation
integrity diversity-inclusion
excellence
service

The larger the word in the word cloud, the more common the word occurred across the companies. What do you notice?

I noticed that "Excellence" was the most common value with "Innovation" and "Diversity-Inclusion" as the second highest.

While this is interesting, the real question is this: "How well are these companies living these values?"

In recent memory, there have been many companies with published values, signs on their walls, and some lip service to try shaping employee behavior only to have their reputations at best, and their entire company at worst, come crashing down because of poor decisions that were in direct conflict with those values.

Arthur Anderson was a large, high-profile accounting firm with a values and mission statement that began with "We believe in integrity..." This former "Big 5" firm's losses and unethical practices led to them issuing internal orders to shred audit materials and other incriminating evidence. Arthur Anderson and many of their largest partners like Enron, imploded publicly.[1] On the flip side, Johnson & Johnson's famous response in 1982 to someone intentionally poisoning bottles of Tylenol is a prime example of how living values guide decision-making to gain (or regain) brand identity and trust. Even though this individual's cyanide-laced pills only impacted people in Illinois, Johnson & Johnson worked with the media and recalled all 31 million bottles worldwide and replaced any bottles already purchased. Their value statement begins, "We believe our first responsibility is to our doctors, nurses and patients, to mothers and fathers, and all others who use our products and services."[2] Their actions were directly aligned with their values, which saved lives, improved innovation, and maintained their brand loyalty.

We all know that publishing values and living them are drastically different. It takes work to define the right values and to consistently reinforce them. Values can create a unified workforce driving the business forward in an aligned and consistent way, so it's worth the effort.

Another positive example of living core values is Chick-fil-A. I will always remember a great 2018 *Entrepreneur* article, "Chick-fil-A Makes More Per Restaurant than McDonald's, Starbucks and Subway Combined...and it's Closed on Sundays." Being closed on Sundays is part of their values to allow employees time to spend with family and friends. The article gives several reasons why this decision actually helps them make more money.[3]

Having a regular and defined cadence of teaching, recognizing, and evaluating company values is imperative for those values to be lived, celebrated, and reinforced. Chick-fil-A has built in a very powerful weekly reminder—being closed on Sunday—of their values. As a thought exercise, think about your organization to see if you can complete the following chart with values teaching or reinforcing activities at each time interval.

Time Frame	Values teaching/reinforcing activity
Weekly	
Monthly	
Quarterly	
Semi-Annually	
Annually	
Ongoing	

If it helps to generate some ideas about what you're already doing or about what you might want to do going forward, here is Guidant's playbook:

Time Frame	Values teaching/reinforcing activity
Weekly	CEO Weekly Email, Monday Morning Stand-up, New-hire onboarding
Monthly	People Newsletter
Quarterly	
Semi-Annually	People Celebration, Town Halls
Annually	Values analysis
Ongoing	Interview questions, values and principles documents available in Employee Resource Center, Microsoft Teams "Cheers"

Because these activities serve important connection purposes that I described in "Chapter 6: Culture Is Connection," most of them are included in the Appendix. I've added explanations below for new ones.

Weekly

- **CEO Weekly Email**. See Appendix.
- **Monday Morning Stand-up**. See Appendix.

- **New-hire onboarding**. We schedule new hires to start on Mondays, and each cohort will attend a thirty-minute discussion on company values and principles. They will learn what they are, then discuss as a group with a facilitator which ones resonate most with them and which one(s) they want to be better at.

Monthly

- **People Newsletter**. See Appendix.

Semi-Annually

- **People Celebration**. See Appendix.
- **Town Halls**. This is something newer that we are testing. The intent is to ask what we're doing well and where we can evolve in three key areas: employee experience, client experience, and company values/principles.

Annually

- **Values analysis**. As part of annual strategic planning with senior leaders, it's important to evaluate how the organization is living up to its core values and principles. Input from the team during town halls can provide helpful information to add to the personal perspective of each senior leader. Considering whether the values and principles are still appropriate is also an important part of this process. At Guidant a few years ago, we changed our value from "Community: Lift each other up" to "Connection: Lift each other up." We felt that

"Connection" better represented our philosophy on culture and better unified us as a fully remote organization so we could be more intentional about living this value.

Ongoing

- **Interview questions**. (More information is provided in "Chapter 2: Hiring for Culture 1– Start Selection with Reflection.") We ensure that interview questions are aligned with the job requirements and company values/principles. For example, for the Adaptability value, we might ask, "Describe a time when you best demonstrated being adaptable at work."
- **Values and principles documents**. These are always accessible and available in the employee resource center.
- **Cheers channel in Microsoft Teams**. See Appendix.

While I prefer "Culture is connection" as a definition of culture, one of my favorite, more traditional definitions is from the *Harvard Business Review*:

"Culture expresses goals through values and beliefs and guides activity through shared assumptions and group norms."[5]

There are many great resources out there for selecting and defining values and principles and striking the right balance between fundamental and aspirational values. *Principles* by Ray Dalio is a powerful book that offers compelling reasons for doing so, along with providing practical tools to achieve it.

"Principles are fundamental truths that serve as foundations for behavior that gets you what you want out of life," Dalio writes. "They can be applied again and again in similar situations to help you achieve your goals."[6]

Instead of spending so much time killing weeds, which in the workplace can look like investing more resources in poor performers instead of top performers, or spending more time on angry customers than ideal customers, or repairing reputational damage caused by poor decisions, we need to be disciplined about spending time growing green grass to prevent these weeds from growing in the first place. We do this by determining, defining, and defending values and principles.

8

The Playbook for a Fully Remote Transition

During my senior year of high school, my dad helped me buy an old manual transmission truck. I hadn't learned to drive a stick shift. The same day we got the truck, my dad left town for a week for work, so he couldn't teach me. On the phone, he told me the basic idea of how to shift, then told me to "Just drive around the neighborhood practicing." I did, which provided immense entertainment for many of our neighbors, given how often, and violently, I stalled that poor little truck.

I quickly learned that at the other extreme, I could peel out, which seemed a much cooler alternative to stalling. So, for the couple of days while I taught myself to drive a stick shift, my friends would gather after school to cheer and laugh as I peeled out four or five times just to get out of the school parking lot and on my way home. Thankfully, with practice, time, and more advice from my dad, I learned to drive a stick shift confidently, and safely.

At present, a talent struggle is taking place between companies and employees. CEOs from prominent companies have recently condemned remote work, making employees all over the globe feel like their work environment is either peeling out or stalling.

Here are a few quotes:

- "I think definitely one of the tech industry's worst mistakes in a long time was that everybody could go full remote forever, and startups didn't need to be together in person and, you know, there was going to be no loss of creativity. I would say that the experiment on that is over, and the technology is not yet good enough that people can be full remote forever, particularly on startups." (Sam Altman, CEO of OpenAI)[1]

- "As I've been meeting with teams throughout the company over the past few months, I've been reminded of the tremendous value in being together with the people you work with. In a creative business like ours, nothing can replace the ability to connect, observe, and create with peers that comes from being physically together, nor the opportunity to grow professionally by learning from leaders and mentors." (Bob Iger, CEO of Disney)[2]

- "I have been unsuccessful, despite everything I've tried to do, to get our people back to work. I've pleaded with them. I said I'll get on my knees. I'll do push-ups. Whatever you want. Come back. No, they are not coming back at the level I want them to. And, you know, we're a very collaborative, creative group. I realize I'm an old-school person, and this is a different generation." Howard Schulz, CEO of Starbucks)[3]

Uncertainty around the future of employee work expectations, and the sincere belief of many people that they are their best when working remotely are causing a major shift in the workforce.

While I admire Howard Schulz's recognition of his own limited view and that there may be genuine nuances with a start-up business as Sam Altman says, I sincerely believe that remote work can work for many organizations. A large pool of talented people is seeking this type of experience where they know they can thrive. At this point, many might say that this is what makes hybrid work the best option (varying combinations of in-office and remote work time). David Nilssen, CEO of Doxa Talent, best describes what I believe: that a hybrid work arrangement exacts a high price from both remote and in-office options and creates too many distractions and limitations to ever realize the full value of either approach.

If stalling or peeling out encapsulates your experience with fully remote work, I hope this playbook will help you think through the different important aspects of this decision and transition: Purpose, Principles, People, and Process.

The first step is to have a clear owner of the project with a committee/task force that supports this individual.

Purpose

- Get clear on the "Why" for the business. What is the primary problem to be solved?
- What is in it for employees?

At Guidant, having some people in the office and some people remote created a lot of complexity for space and tools. This created a very different meeting experience for someone who was remote compared to three people who were in the office together. Challenges include side talk, poor audio, and being left out of conversations. Moving to fully remote helped the business and team members have more effective and consistent communication experiences while drastically reducing our costs for office space.

"What's in it for employees?" should be the focus of two-way communication. Understanding what they are most excited about, then establishing a consistent talk track will help bring clarity, reassurance, and excitement. No commutes, all team members on an equal playing field, able to relocate, recruiting better talent, etc.

At Guidant, we estimate that we save up to eight hundred thousand miles on the roads every year for our 125 U.S. team members. This statistic resonated with many environmentally conscious team members and those who appreciate that fewer miles means less gas money, less pollution, less traffic frustration, less road wear, and more personal time.

Principles

Define principles for going fully remote. These should help answer the many questions that lie ahead, including those in this chapter under the subheadings "People" and "Process." After considering our existing company values and principles, we at Guidant are proud of the following additional remote principles we established to help shape our focus:

- Culture is connection. (See "Chapter 6: Culture Is Connection" for additional information, measurements, and tools.)
- People have different expectations and connection needs. We'll provide a menu.

- Let's consider this a great experiment and invite the company to lean into testing and learning. Be okay with the unknown.
- Remote work isn't for everyone. Let's accept that some great team members may leave.
- We value the team's perspective. We'll seek feedback early and often.

Your principles will probably look different. Consider company values and principles and how applying them to the experience of remote work will help formulate additional principles to shape the process.

People

- **Seek employees' perspectives**. Ask them what they like about working remotely, what they're nervous about, how effective they think they are or will be, overall engagement, most important connection opportunities or collaboration tools, and so on.
- **Create a code of conduct**. Set clear expectations for working and interacting. Common practices include a quiet space, how to show up at meetings, internet connection speed, dress code, meeting host responsibilities, a "cameras on" expectation, and other topics. At Guidant, we include information about which U.S. states employees can relocate to, encouragement to take care of themselves physically and mentally with clear work/life boundaries, and where to find other helpful resources.
- **Develop a thoughtful communication plan**. Who will communicate what, to whom, when, and how often? There is value in telling stories

about the purpose of the change and how the company, clients, and team members all benefit from it. We chose to overcommunicate and lean into transparency. We often got feedback from team members saying that they really appreciated this approach because we were making these changes during the very uncertain beginnings of the COVID-19 pandemic.

- **Evaluate current hiring, onboarding, and training processes.** Determine what may need to shift with this change—for example, job postings, ensuring candidates can access the right hardware (camera), guiding them on how to use the software (video conferencing) to participate. This is a great time to test simplifying processes and to introduce more effective and efficient methods.
- **Understand and address what will likely be the three main employee questions/concerns**: Collaboration, Connection, Compensation.
  - Collaboration
    - How will we be as effective at collaboration?
    - What will one-on-ones, team meetings, and all-company meetings be like?
    - What tools will we use now? There are several solutions or workarounds available for shifting any current tools to those that may be most effective for a remote workforce.
  - Connection
    - How will I connect with my team members?
    - What current activities stay, what goes away, what gets tested?

- How will we approach any in-person events/activities?
- How will I get interaction with senior leaders?
- How will we regularly and effectively live, share, and recognize company values?

○ Compensation

- If the company has more money, will I get paid more?
- Where can I move, and will that impact my pay? The company should be very proactive and very clear about this. Different states have wildly different business tax requirements and employment laws. (See the Appendix for information on how Guidant approaches this.)
- What equipment do I pay for, and what does the company pay for? Be ready to answer questions about desks, chairs, office supplies, internet, and computer accessories. Some U.S. states have requirements for this, and others are considering introducing them. Be sure to understand what is required in the states the company currently operates in and those where it intends to.

Process

Make time to tackle major decisions. While they are listed innocuously here, they will take significant investment for discussion, decision, execution, and evaluation:

- **Timing**. Decide who, what, when, and where. Shift in phases or all at once? Test just one team before moving on or transition the whole team? What roles will be needed to facilitate different elements of the team like who oversees communication, logistics, technology, etc.?

- **Technology**. List all technology currently being used. Determine which ones are necessary to continue working remotely, which can be eliminated, and what additional solutions are needed. For example, everyone who didn't have a webcam before will need one now, phone systems and copy machines might be eliminated, and the same email solution might still work.

- **One hundred percent electronic files and operations**. Whatever isn't fully electronic will likely have to be going forward. This includes employee files, document signatures, training, and many other elements of the employee experience, plus operations. Similarly, there will need to be a place to store/present information such as employment law posters, job descriptions, company information, etc. I've used both Dropbox and Microsoft Teams for this purpose and been happy with both.

- **Define metrics that matter and measure them**. Before a major change, it's important to establish a baseline of core metrics to understand what is going well and where shifts might need to be made. This is particularly helpful for testing different ideas, so regular feedback can either validate the test or allow a quick course correction. Traditional metrics like engagement and retention are important. We also introduced questions such as, "How effective are you at working remotely?"

- **Physical office exit**. Someone will need to coordinate the ending of a lease, utilities, and contracts (copier for example). Additional steps include cleaning, inspections, and distributing all remaining office items. We did this successfully by assigning a single point of contact to oversee the entire process. They had a silent auction for the larger items, then over one weekend had people come to pick up winning auction items and anything else in the office for free—books, small furniture, dishes, tools, etc.

- **Physical address**. Google basically requires a physical address to verify a business for reviews and other search engine optimization purposes. Mail will still need to be received at a PO box so someone will need to check it regularly or partner with a mail scanning service to do this.

If you're still on the fence, remember that while remote work may introduce some different challenges to tackle, it resolves what seems to be a never-ending battle over dishes—who left dishes in the sink? Whose turn is it to wash them? What humorous (yet condescending) sign should we put in the kitchen to remind people they're adults? If you've solved the dishes problem at your workplace, please write a book. I'll buy YOUR book.

What also goes away: Body odors and overpowering perfumes, that one person who is a pen clicker, the corn nuts or crispy carrots eater, the toenail clipper, and other people's cat and dog hair. Goodbye to fights over temperature, music volume and genres, and awkward bathroom encounters.

At the risk of dating this book quickly, here are some tools/partners that I have personally used, and can recommend, to maximize the remote experience. Even though their functions or names may change in the future, this should still provide a good starting place to explore these or similar options.

- Connection: Microsoft Teams including channels, Yammer groups, Zoom, Airbnb online experiences, Kudoboards, Let's Roam
- Food: Grubhub corporate account—for an event or meeting everyone gets money in their account to spend through Grubhub
- Surveys: Survey Monkey
- Swag: SwagUp
- Electronic signatures: DocuSign
- Physical mail management: Earth Class Mail
- Applicant Tracking System: Workable

There are significant advantages to remote work that outweigh the supposed or actual challenges. I can now drive a stick shift car and, by using this playbook, we can all confidently transition to fully remote without stalling or peeling out.

9

Seattle Mariners or Colorado Rockies

One of my favorite training methods is to tell a story and have the audience extract the lessons from the story itself. This is most effective at the beginning of a presentation before the participants know too much about what you'll be saying on the topic. This lack of initial information leaves them free to think about the story in a way that's most meaningful for them. I like to say, "I'll tell the story, you tell me your takeaways." Storytelling in this way also provides some initial discussion that is usually easy to build on, regardless of the direction of the actual presentation.

I'm going to demonstrate that in this chapter with a story that I believe has many possible interpretations, lessons to learn, and perspectives. Some may even take away conflicting interpretations, which further highlights the value of this method.

My great friend, Jason Fletcher, is a lifelong Seattle Mariners fan. In fact, they are the same age. He was born the same year the Mariners were formed, and they are the closest Major League Baseball Team to the area where he grew up. The Mariners have neither won a World Series nor even made it to a World Series. One day, Jason said something that made me laugh out loud at the time, and deeply ponder ever since.

He said, "When does loyalty become stupidity?"

Because we both share a love for baseball, we became fast friends, and he is the reason, being one of the owners of Ashley Manor and Auburn Crest Hospice, I later came on board as the Human Resources director there. He jokes that he "rescued me from local government."

Throughout the six years I had the privilege of working with him, we had many opportunities to travel around our company footprint visiting our assisted living and hospice locations and the team members there. Traveling occasionally took us within range to catch home games of the Seattle Mariners and the Colorado Rockies. In fact, we normally had the flexibility to plan our trips around their schedules.

We each enjoyed meeting players while getting autographs and taking pictures with them, when we had the chance. I have a shelf in my office with many signed baseballs, each with a wonderful memory. We liked to get to games early to enjoy the baseball atmosphere, watch batting practice, and see if any players were signing autographs. In doing this, we noticed vastly different approaches each baseball club took in managing fans. See if you can spot some of the differences.

In Colorado, there is a literal yellow line painted on the steps at row eleven for all sections behind home plate and up around both dugouts, which is where most players will come to interact with fans. Even two hours before the game, nobody was allowed in these seats unless they had a ticket. Even kids who just wanted a closer look behind home plate, or a couple who wanted to take a picture, had to have a ticket, or they weren't allowed to go beyond the yellow line. Here is the actual description from their website:

Autographs

"...(G)uests are permitted to seek autographs from players along the railing between Sections 116-121 and 142-146 up to 40 minutes prior to game time, or until the end of batting practice, whichever comes first. Please be considerate by not inconveniencing Guests seated in these areas...(G)uests wishing to watch batting practice in the area behind home plate from dugout to dugout may sit or stand from row 11 to the concourse. Only those Guests with tickets for rows 1-10 will be permitted into those seats."

"Once the batting cage is removed from the home plate area, we ask for your cooperation in returning to your ticketed seat...Items should not be given to Colorado Rockies staff members, or taken to the Guest Relations Center or the Colorado Rockies main offices in order to attempt to obtain autographs from players or media/broadcast personnel."[1]

To enforce this rule, the Rockies employed around twenty people, about one per section, to stand all along the yellow line to only allow ticket holders. We once asked one of the people standing guard the reason for the yellow line, and they said it was a policy to "protect the safety of the players and the fans." Having interactions with Rockies players are limited, and this group of twenty employees spends up to two hours before each game checking tickets and telling a lot of kids and adults that they can't cross the yellow line. Some interactions were rude on both sides and, in one situation, potentially dangerous. We witnessed an employee, a man probably in his seventies, trying to chase some kids out of the area around the seats and up the stairs. Thankfully, nobody was injured at our game.

Now, let's look at how this works in Seattle. Here is what their autograph policy says: Nothing. They don't have one. In fact, the four to six employees who are around the home plate and dugout area often call over to kids in the stands when a player stops to sign autographs. Every time we went, we literally saw these employees, all probably in their sixties or seventies (awesome part-time job!), crawling over the dugout with fan items in their hands to give to the players, then returning the autographed items to the appropriate fans. The result: 75 percent fewer employees needed, more players signing autographs, and more fans interacting with players and getting autographs. I didn't witness anything that I would have considered a risk to the players and fans.

What takeaways do you have from this story? How can you take what you've extracted and apply it to yourself, your family, or your work?

Even though it's obvious where my ballpark experience preference lands, there's a lot to consider here from a business and Human Resources perspective: staffing, rules, risks, customer experience, battles to fight, and resource allocation. It's also important to consider the preferred experience of autograph seekers compared to the experience of fans with great seats who don't want autographs and may have their view blocked. Each company had values they had established and were trying to live by.

This has influenced how I think about certain rules we have with our children and my philosophy on the right way to trust people working remotely.

So who do you agree with? Who has it right?

Seattle Mariners or Colorado Rockies

Circle one of the above, and note your reasons:

_____

_____

_____

_____

I hope this was a helpful exercise and that this method of storytelling is something you can try in your next training, presentation, or strategic planning discussions.

10

Death by Acronyms

Have you ever noticed that different industries seem to have their own language? The military, healthcare, technology, etc., all have unique phrases, terminology, and, especially, acronyms. It can sometimes be hard for people outside those circles to understand the dialogue.

One time, when I was working for the hospice company, a caring daughter asked to see a nurse's recent notes regarding their mother and was appalled at seeing that the nurse had written her mother was "a little S.O.B." Understandably, she was furious. It took some explanation and patience for this upset daughter to accept that this was shorthand for "a little shortness of breath."

The question "When was your last BM [bowel movement]?" must have become so repetitive for some patient that my family once saw "Last BM?" as graffiti on a large rock face entering a canyon in Utah.

The use of unfamiliar language caused me to see some things that I cannot unsee.

When I first started working for the hospice and assisted living company, I felt like I was learning a foreign language. I had to become familiar with phrases like "instant in-service," regulatory government entities like CMS (Centers for Medicare & Medicaid Services), and how the word *census* was used to describe clients, plus a host of medical terms.

In just my second week on the job, we had our weekly leadership team meeting, and I was desperate to be fluent in the language quickly. So when someone mentioned an issue with a resident with MRSA, I googled it. I saw images that are etched in my brain forever, showing rashes in places only a doctor and a partner should see. Ever.

I've noticed that in Human Resources, where we should be the stewards of the employee work experience, we are some of the worst offenders. Specifically with Human Resources, someone might hear a sentence like this:

"If you have questions about PTO, FMLA, or COBRA see your BP in HR and they can show you in our HRIS where to get information for your SDR role on the BizDev team."

We must have forgotten what it is like to not understand what people are saying and how demoralizing and embarrassing that can be for team members, especially those who are new.

Here's an exercise you can try:

In your next all-company meeting of any kind, hopefully with some new team members included, make a list of every acronym, jargon word, titles for anything that has more than one name, and anything that is part of the company or any industry nomenclature that's mentioned without explanation. Or, if you're adventurous, ask a brave new hire to attend a meeting and have them do this exercise.

My guess is you'll be very surprised how extensive the list is. I hope we can remember the feelings and emotions we have when this happens to us and have empathy for our team members who might be experiencing this in our organizations.

When I first joined Guidant Financial, I noticed that a single department was interchangeably called: 401k, Plan Administration, Client Services, Client Contact, Operations, the backend, Recordkeeping, or just RK. We also had a weekly meeting with everyone that we called Monday Morning Stand-up, all-company meeting, weekly meeting, and many other combinations of Monday, Stand-up, meeting, weekly, and company. It took a couple of confusing months for me to reconcile this. Now, we have the 401k Administration Services team and the Monday Morning Stand-up (MMSU) that permeates all our documents, language, and presentations.

Okay, so that's a lot of examples. What do we do about it? Let's take the lead to fix it. Here are some ideas:

- Keep noticing the acronyms, jargon, and unique words in our work vocabulary to make people aware of them. Complete that exercise as often as needed. Awareness is the first big step.
- Create a single name for every department, job title, process, system, etc., and stick to it. That will require communicating this intention, discipline for sticking to it, and a champion to remind people.
- In PowerPoint presentations, email messages, word documents, and other forms of communication, there is usually room to write out the name instead of an acronym.
- The proper way to use an acronym in writing is to first write the full name with the acronym in parentheses. Then, you can use that acronym

throughout that message or document. For example, on the Human Resources (HR) team, there are often HR business partners to support the organization.

- Take an extra sentence to explain any jargon or words unique to the company.
- Provide time and safety for new team members to ask questions about anything they hear that is new to them. A "partner in crime" type onboarding program is perfect for this.

Even with the passion I have for this issue, I must admit that it takes ongoing focus to be effective. In just the last few months, I have had to explain what the acronym MMSU stands for during an international speaking opportunity, and I had a new employee tell me that she didn't have the "all-company meeting" that I messaged her about on her calendar—because her calendar showed Monday Morning Stand-up, not anything about an all-company meeting. I knew better!

I recognize that acronyms and specific nomenclatures have value and a place in our language. In fact, I use several acronyms as helpful mnemonic devices in this book because they make concepts easier to remember and apply. Even the book title is an acronym! In the spirit of creating great culture and work experiences, speaking a common language is a core foundation. Let us take up the challenge to do our part in simplifying and explaining our thoughts in a better way. Considering our audience and practice are two great steps.

SECTION 3

Upleveling Leadership

11

The Silver Bullet in Leadership*

*There is no silver bullet in leadership.

I know this because I've looked. I've read amazing books, attended exceptional conferences, had outstanding mentors, practiced best principles, and met world-renowned leaders. I have learned a tremendous amount from these experiences. Most importantly, I learned that there is no single perfect way to lead. For me, that realization was both exciting and scary. While there is no silver bullet in leadership, regular and effective one-on-one meetings are as close as it comes.

Leaders occasionally struggle with a team member on performance, attendance, or behavior. Even when the team member is doing well, a good supervisor will want to see how to help keep them engaged and growing. I have frequent conversations with leaders in these situations, and I'm grateful they find it helpful to talk through how to approach the situation. After learning about the challenge they're facing, my first question is usually "Tell me about the quality and frequency of your one-on-ones with this team member."

I've found a high correlation between the quality of a work relationship and the quality and frequency of one-on-one meetings.

High-quality relationships provide the fertile ground for us to be highly effective leaders. In fact, one of my favorite quotes from the book *Primal Leadership* by Daniel Goleman comes right from the Preface, "The fundamental task of leaders, we argue, is to prime good feeling in those they lead. That occurs when a leader creates resonance—a reservoir of positivity that frees the best in people."[1]

At a company I consulted for, I once had a senior leader come to me because they were struggling to get along with their direct supervisor, who was the CEO. They explained that they felt unsupported and disrespected. After asking about some specific examples that made them feel that way, I asked, "Tell me about the quality and frequency of your one-on-one meetings."

They said, "We don't have one-on-one meetings."

"In the last year that you have reported to this person, you've never had a one-on-one meeting?"

"The only time we meet one-on-one is impromptu and when one of us is already upset about something. It seems they only want to talk to me when they think I've screwed something up."

Let's pause there. Have you ever felt that way? Might there be people on your team or in your company who might feel that way? These were very smart, very educated, and very accomplished professionals who were struggling to interact with each other under the natural pressures of business and leadership. It might seem easy to prioritize tasks over people.

The senior leader recognized how meeting regularly one-on-one in a planned, proactive way would help. They told me, "I'm going to suggest that we start meeting weekly."

Here's why effective one-on-ones are so powerful: First, think about all the exciting opportunities and responsibilities we have as leaders: training, seeking feedback, reviewing performance, setting and monitoring goals, evaluating metrics, delegating, providing recognition, coaching on behavior or performance, generating accountability, gaining clarity on priorities, building relationships, and others. All these important activities can happen during an effective one-on-one meeting.

This is particularly useful for proactively managing performance. Some supervisors prefer what I call the "sock of pennies" method—slowly adding a penny inside a sock every time their team member makes a mistake—quietly hoping performance or behavior will improve on its own, until the sock is so full and heavy that they go swinging it angrily to pummel that employee with a pile of grievances from the past six months all at once. With effective one-on-ones, we can regularly and comfortably talk about what is going well and what might need a minor adjustment in behavior or performance closer to real-time and usually before either person hits a breaking point.

In fact, I surveyed our team to discover what issues they find most helpful to discuss in their one-on-one meetings:

guidance   **challenges**

goals

performance

questions   feedback

support   personal

Notice that people genuinely want to discuss their performance—good and bad—to receive feedback from their direct supervisor and talk about challenges they're facing so they can perform now and get better over time.

Let's self-assess how we're doing right now with all our direct reports. Below are ten elements of effective one-on-one meetings. See how you're doing overall and where you might improve:

Rating scale:

5 – Excellent
4 – Very Good
3 – Good
2 – Not Very Good
1 – Poor

#	Effective 1:1 Elements	Score 1-5
1	Hold 1:1s with each direct report at least monthly	
2	1:1s are set up as recurring meetings in an electronic calendar	
3	Not canceling or rescheduling 1:1s	
4	Using an agenda (visible ahead of time, both can add to it	
5	Discussing performance and providing feedback	
6	Allowing space for some personal connection	
7	Providing time for team members to share perspectives, ideas, challenges	

8	Saving/documenting the agenda or meeting notes	
9	Following up on prior commitments	
10	Focused during the meeting—eye contact, not checking devices or doing other work	
TOTAL		

Pick one or two elements to improve. Take this self-assessment again in sixty days to see how you can celebrate improvements and discover the next place to improve.

BONUS: Take this assessment for the one-on-one meetings you have with your direct supervisor. See if there is an area that would help you feel more productive, valued, or heard, and see if you can make suggestions to improve the effectiveness of those meetings.

So far, we've focused on the responsibility of the supervisor. It's important that both people know their role, which might look something like this:

Supervisors ensure	**Employees prepared to**
• At least monthly • Set date/time on a recurring calendar • Mechanism for maintaining an agenda together, taking notes, keeping track of commitments, following up, and getting feedback	• Review performance • Receive and provide feedback • Discuss goals • Share ideas and support needs

Here is a brief structure of my meetings:

1. Have the team member decide the frequency and length, as long as it's at least thirty minutes per month. I also let them decide the day of the week, and I prioritize my schedule around them. I have a different cadence with each team member.
2. Meetings are set as recurring calendar invitations.
3. In Microsoft Teams, we have a shared agenda that we both add topics to at any time.
4. We always have an icebreaker at the beginning. (Google and ChatGPT have thousands.) I prefer to ask the same each time: What did you do well in the last week? What are you most excited about next week? Who have you seen live our values that we can recognize?
5. We discuss performance, metrics, wins, challenges, improvement opportunities, prior commitments, two-way feedback, new commitments, etc.
6. I save that day's agenda in my personal folders (Your future self will love you come annual performance review time)
7. Repeat!

The direct supervisor relationship is the most important relationship at work. In fact, a recent study concluded that direct supervisors (or managers) have more impact on employees' mental health than their therapist and the same amount as their partner.[2] When we step into leadership, we step onto sacred ground.

The importance of this relationship was solidified for me years ago when I worked with the memory care company. We wanted to improve our retention of caregivers in the sixty-plus memory care communities we had in three states. We knew retention was a key to great resident care, so we wanted to put in energy and effort to help caregivers feel valued. As an executive team, we spent a lot of time brainstorming and implementing ideas. In the first ninety days, we introduced various activities. Our CEO, Keith Fletcher, would visit every location personally, our vice presidents of operations would call every new team member after their first week to introduce themselves and check on their experience so far. We sent welcome gifts with fun branded items and new scrubs. My team called people on their birthday, introduced more flexible shifts, along with many other such initiatives.

We learned a powerful lesson: A company, or senior leaders, can only amplify an already positive experience with a direct supervisor and can never replace it. The result on retention: surprisingly and disappointingly, much less than we hoped. We had so many wonderful administrators who were the state-licensed managers of each memory care community, and we had some who struggled to be great leaders in that role. It's a tough job. The locations that experienced an improvement in retention already had a great administrator who had good relationships with their team. When the administrators had not yet established such relationships, we had little improvement in our retention efforts at those locations. We learned we needed to focus on the direct supervisor relationship first.

I'll repeat: The direct supervisor relationship is the most important relationship at work. I believe the best opportunity to be the best leader we can be is to have regular and effective one-on-one meetings with each team member.

Let's go back to the senior leader and their CEO. After only a month of having regularly scheduled one-on-one meetings, each individual came to me independently to tell me about the drastic improvement they were seeing in their relationship and outcomes. I heard phrases about them being aligned, being open, laughing together, discussing challenging topics respectfully, and overall feeling better about being at work and contributing.

Because this is such a high-leverage activity, I expect any investment you make in improving the quality and effectiveness of your one-on-ones will see immediate and long-term returns.

12

E.A.S.E. into More Effectiveness

My parents, siblings, and our spouses once had a wonderful vacation in the Turks and Caicos. We love snorkeling, so we took an excursion with a guide. After snorkeling in a couple of locations, the plan was to anchor the boat in an area abundant with queen conch to dive down and pick our own to eat. Our guide would then take us to an uninhabited island where he would personally make a fresh conch salad on the spot.

As we arrived at our diving location, we excitedly hopped off the boat and began surveying the underwater area to find conch to catch. We dispersed around the boat, and I ended up near my older sister, Melissa. I found my target first and dove around twelve feet to grab the conch shell. As I surfaced, Melissa said, "I see mine!" and then furiously kicked her feet to get down to the ocean floor. Her legs stayed elevated out of the water, rapidly kicking the air the whole time. She never went fully underwater, much less anywhere near the conch. She righted herself, took a deep breath, then again plunged barely underwater, again with her feet flying wildly in the air. Determined, she earnestly tried a third time with the same result, not able to even come close to reaching the conch shells on the bottom. She floated there, huffing and puffing from the strenuous effort for a moment, then exasperatedly said to me, "I CAN'T GET ONE!"

She then noticed that I was laughing so hard that I almost dropped my own conch shell. Now exhausted and confused, she said, "What?!?" In between laughs, I pointed to her and said, "Melissa, you're wearing a life jacket!" As she realized what happened and how funny that must have been for those watching, we laughed so hard, and we still laugh today when we remember this story. She had me hold her life jacket while she dived, finally getting her conch shell.

Many parts of our lives, many decisions we've made, and elements of our work serve us well. Still, like my sister's life jacket, it's important to take time to evaluate which areas are still serving us well and which areas might actually be holding us back.

I've developed a framework to help me evaluate shifts I can make to ensure I'm focusing on the most important and most impactful areas of my work and up-leveling my team along the way. I call this framework E.A.S.E. into Effectiveness. Are you looking to stay scrappy, scale a company or service, make a bigger impact, or spend more time on the most important areas that also bring you energy? Welcome to E.A.S.E: Eliminate, Automate, Simplify, Empower.

Eliminate

I have made Eliminate the first step on purpose. If we can truly eliminate something from our work, this will create immediate benefits. Also, we won't spend our time or energy in the subsequent steps on something that we can stop doing altogether. In a great irreverent book called *Up the Organization: How to Stop the Corporation from Stifling People and Strangling Profits,* author Robert Townsend has a chapter called "Vice President of Killing Things."[1] The idea is that we become good at eliminating and feel empowered and excited by doing it.

Here are some examples of tasks that I have eliminated:

- **Signatures on some forms**. Does the CEO or HR leader need to sign everything?
- **Responding to every salesperson**. To be kind, I once tried to respond to every salesperson's call or email. When I realized it would be a part-time job to do so, I stopped.
- **Meetings**. Some were no longer necessary, or I was no longer adding or getting value, so I respectfully removed myself from them.
- **Saying yes to everything**. Saying no upfront is an important way of proactively eliminating commitments that might otherwise interfere with more important responsibilities. (See "Chapter 16: The 95 Percent Principle, Future Cory, and Other Prioritization Tools" for how to do this well.)
- **Programs**. I once ended employee of the month and employee recognition programs after a few months as the HR director at the healthcare company. I'm sure people at first thought, "What kind of people leader would end these recognition programs?" Answer: One who knew we could find simpler and easier ways to recognize others sincerely without a program and knew we needed to focus our limited

resources on more important areas. Also, these programs often caused more friction and conflict than the good feelings they were intended to create. Here's a test: the next time you are in any place that has an Employee of the Month program proudly displayed on a wall, I'll send you five dollars if they are still current with the right month, and you send me five dollars if they are behind. While I'm joking, I think I would have ended up with a lot of money ahead.

- **Processes**. At the healthcare company, we also had a process where team members could purchase scrubs through the company. In my first couple of weeks, I was there trying to listen to everyone I could and I think I heard more complaints about this than anything else. Gone.

Automate

Areas where we spend a lot of time or spend small amounts of time repeatedly are excellent targets for automation. Many tools and resources can help us do this. Here are a few areas that I've automated:

- **Benefits enrollments**. We've partnered with the right companies and spent the time upfront to automate this process. Finding long-term partners can really help.
- **Macros in Microsoft Excel**. I run monthly reports to analyze and present different metrics, which requires me to run the same reports and take the same actions each month. This is the perfect place to record the actions being taken through a macro, which essentially operates like a recording, so the next time you have data and run that macro it will repeat those same steps.

- **Reports**. I currently run monthly reports from our payroll system. There is a feature there where I can create custom reports, if needed, and then also create a schedule for that report to be run and sent to me at a certain time on a certain day every month.
- **Email rules**. I have different folders to capture different emails automatically. I've set rules for certain senders to go to a different folder that I know I can check less regularly than my normal inbox. This keeps me organized, focused, and with more energy. I know some people create a rule to have any email they are carbon copied (cc'd) on go to a separate folder so they can focus on emails written directly to them.
- **Templates are an excellent form of automation**. I've created email templates for emails that I send regularly, such as welcoming a candidate who just signed an offer letter. We also have templates for PowerPoint presentations, different email notifications, and forms. If it's a repeated task, it's worth considering a template. I like to say, "Templatize your life," as this preserves already invested energy and conserves future energy.

Simplify

If something cannot be eliminated or automated, we can regain our energy and calendars by simplifying. Here are a few ideas:

- **Instead of having typical thirty and sixty-minute meetings, schedule twenty-five and fifty-minute meetings**. People will love you for it, and on a day packed with meetings, so will your bladder.

- **Check the employee handbook**. I suspect an honest look at our employee handbooks will reveal areas we can simplify. We'll likely have overexplained many areas where less would be more. For example, since the handbook is aimed at current team members, I've removed any references to policies about candidates. I've also removed and stored benefits-specific content in a separate place solely for our benefits materials.

- **When I first joined Guidant, part of the annual performance review and merit increase process was a three-day calibration marathon** where each supervisor received feedback from other leaders on each of their team members. All company leaders discussed and debated performance, experiences, and perspectives to get alignment on how every single team member was viewed by all the leaders in the company. Then each supervisor distributed a pool of dollars based on these ratings and rankings. This often resulted in many different amounts being used for each person. For example, on a single team, Person A might receive a 3.21 percent increase, Person B might receive 3.05 percent, and Person C might receive 2.94 percent, all for the same performance rating. In my first year, we implemented three performance rating options, with the rating determined by the direct supervisor and reviewed with Human Resources, and each rating had a specific merit increase percentage. Depending on the year, this might be a 4.5 percent increase for exceeding expectations, a 3 percent increase for meeting expectations, and a 1.5 percent increase for performing below expectations. Many years later, I still have people thank me for simplifying our process because it was time-consuming, confusing, and exhausting.

- **Rethink reference checks**. We've simplified our hiring process by changing how we think about reference checks. Depending upon the role, we either skip this step entirely or we take a different approach. (See "Chapter 27: Traditional HR vs. HR Evolutions" for more.)

Empower

If we want, eliminating, automating, and simplifying can be done on our own. Empower is where we must maximize other people's contributions and development. A great book on this topic is called *Who Not How* by Dr. Benjamin Hardy and Dan Sullivan. The fundamental and brilliantly simple approach is changing our question from "How can I accomplish this?" to "Who can help me achieve this?"[2] This is a great mindset to use to empower others. Here's one idea for empowering others (see more in "Chapter 13: Delegate Like a Boss"):

- **Employee Resource Center**. My past two organizations have been complex companies–healthcare and finance. Incredible amounts of information are needed to run these businesses effectively. I'm proud to have set up an Employee Resource Center in both companies. I realized that many questions we get in Human Resources are simple and routine: What does this policy say? Which holidays do we have off? Where can

I find our company values? Where can I get the forms for a Family and Medical Leave Act (FMLA) leave request?

Before the creation of an Employee Resource Center, the answers to these and a thousand other questions were stored in different folders, emails, people's heads, and some interesting urban legends. In creating an Employee Resource Center (On Dropbox at one company, and Microsoft Teams at another), we set up a centralized, easy-to-access, always up-to-date form/document that was read-only for all users so everything stayed that way. This empowered our team to seek answers to most of their questions. It's a better experience for them because they don't have to wait on another person, and a better experience for other team members who can stay focused on other priorities.

E.A.S.E. into Effectiveness has also served me well in my personal life. I have eliminated relationships and iPhone apps that were no longer serving me, automated as many bills as possible, simplified my commitments to those most meaningful to me right now, and empowered my kids to take on more responsibility.

Below is a great exercise to use with a family or a team. To create more time for the aspects of our life we enjoy most and where we can make the biggest impact, set time aside to ask these questions generally, or related to a specific process like the hiring process.

Here's one way to do it:

1. Set aside thirty to forty-five minutes with a team ahead of time. Ask them to come prepared to answer the questions below and act on the stated strategies.

2. If you had four more hours in your work week, how would you enjoy spending it adding more value? (Notice that enjoy and adding value are both key here.)
3. Where in the past have we seen great success in eliminating, automating, simplifying, and empowering? Talk through each one.
4. Let's brainstorm all the places where we can now eliminate, automate, simplify, and empower.
5. Let's vote and find the top three ideas to work on in the next week.
6. Track it. Report back at the next team meeting.
7. Repeat steps 4 to 6 regularly.

Complexity constantly enters our lives without us noticing. Whether we've had resources cut, we're preparing for significant growth at scale, or we need a spring cleaning of our function, we must regularly combat this complexity. When something goes wrong, our first instinct is often to add another step to audit or check so it doesn't happen again. This is how complexity and inefficiency begin. If our instincts were to apply the E.A.S.E. method instead, we would usually find a better and more efficient solution.

I hereby declare you the Vice President of Killing Things. Keep your life jacket on if it's still serving you. Otherwise, see how satisfying it is to take an hour of your time diving in on what you can eliminate, automate, simplify, or empower. Write them down here:

Eliminate	
Automate	

| Simplify | |
| Empower | |

13

Delegate Like a Boss

Benjamin Zander, the conductor of the Boston Philharmonic Orchestra, said, "The conductor doesn't make a sound. He depends for his power on his ability to make other people powerful. My job is to awaken possibility in other people."[1] Think about this powerful quote and how it relates to our roles working with people.

A few years ago, I was wrestling with the idea of heading into my forties when I found myself getting a haircut at Great Clips. I love Great Clips because it's a combination of grooming and gambling—it costs fifteen dollars and a figurative roll of the dice. Sometimes I love my haircut, and sometimes I lose the bet. I do sincerely appreciate the price, location, and walk-in convenience. As I sat with a stylist who was new to me, I wondered how my haircut would turn out. She was in her early twenties, had an awesome pink mohawk, and was very friendly. I was happy with the cut—she did a really great job on my hair.

As she was wrapping up, she spun me around, looked at me, and asked, "Do you want me to trim your eyebrows?" Nobody had ever asked me that before!

Surprised, I could only muster a quick, nervous laugh and a feeble answer, "Oh, do they need it?" Without dignifying her response with words, she simply cocked her head and pink mohawk to the side and raised her own eyebrows as high as she could, which I assume meant, "Are you joking?" I gave another quick laugh, shrugged my shoulders, and said, "I guess if you're willing to ask, I need to be willing to try it."

She trimmed them down, and I thought they looked good. When I got home, I was laughing about the whole experience as I explained the situation to my wife. I told her about the stylist, my haircut, and how she was brave enough to ask if I wanted my eyebrows trimmed. My wife immediately interjected, "Why didn't you let her?!" That made me laugh even harder. Clearly, I needed to let go of my aging concerns and embrace the fact that I needed to take care of myself differently by taming apparently wild eyebrows—something that everyone else but me seemed to notice.

Letting go and changing can be hard. In my experience, when I ask leaders which leadership skills they want to develop, many of them identify delegation. In this chapter, I'm going to share some of the best examples I know to help us let go and "Delegate Like a Boss."

First, let's talk about what I mean by "delegation," because I have heard some terrible definitions. I once heard someone describe delegation as "Find what you hate doing the most, and get anyone else to do it for you."

Here is my personally crafted definition: "A mutually beneficial, long-term leadership activity where one individual effectively shifts the responsibility of an important outcome to another."

Read that sentence again, and see which words resonate with you. Just reflecting on this explanation should help you start to develop ideas on applying it. I hope people take away keywords with this understanding:

- **Mutual**. This must benefit both people involved, not just the person delegating.
- **Long-term**. Delegation is an investment in both your futures. If you need somebody to pick up lunch, respond to an email, or make a few copies, that is okay and necessary sometimes. Let's just stop calling that delegation; it's an assignment.
- **Effectively**. There are lots of ways to do this poorly. You've probably been delegated to poorly in your career, so you know what this looks and feels like. Delegation must be effective.
- **Responsibility**. The responsibility shifts. We can't pretend to delegate and then micromanage. It's only delegation if we focus on the outcome and leave flexibility on the method. We might have strong opinions about how to achieve the outcome, but the new person responsible will only grow if there is some autonomy on how to achieve the results. This is where we let go.
- **Important outcome**. It's only delegation if it's important.

I once did a delegation workshop where I asked participants to define delegation in just five words. There were some remarkable responses. Here is my favorite: "Multiplying ourselves by developing others." Try this exercise with yourself or with your team. How would you define delegation in five words?

Now, let's establish a powerful reason for us to delegate. My friend Jason Fletcher wants to grow his business and delegate so well that he can take a thirty-day vacation and no one will notice. That is powerful and motivating! Here are some questions to ask yourself to find the inspiration and purpose to put forth the necessary effort to do this well:

- As I encouraged you to ask in "Chapter 12: E.A.S.E. into More Effectiveness," if you suddenly had four extra hours open in your work week every week, how would you spend them? Note that this isn't about adding four hours to your work week—it's as if every Friday morning from 8 a.m. to 12:00 p.m. was suddenly wide open. How would you spend this time?
- How does the definition of delegation in this chapter align with your company's core values and principles? How might this align with your personal and leadership values and principles?
- How might your team benefit most from you being able to delegate better?
- What is the biggest benefit for you from being able to delegate better?

Here are some facts that might also motivate us. My teenage son often says, "That's facts" or just "Facts." So, here you go. Facts:

- As of this writing, there are over ten million jobs open in the United States.[2]
- In January 2023, 61 percent of workers in the United States were considering leaving their job, including 76 percent of Generation Z

and millennials.[3] Millennials are the largest generation in the workforce right now.[4]

- The global pandemic opened people's minds about their work, and of those contemplating changing companies, 80 percent were doing so because of career growth.[5] They are looking elsewhere to improve their careers because this wasn't happening at their existing workplace.
- Ken Chenault, former CEO of American Express, reportedly spent up to 50 percent of his time on talent management. Oh, and at one point in his American Express career journey, he grew a troubled merchandising operation from $150 million in sales to $500 million.[6]

The leaders and companies that provide these growth opportunities by delegating well are best positioned to attract, retain, and promote top talent.

Delegation Process

I've broken down the delegation process into four sequential steps. Each builds on the prior step and can then be repeated to continue a virtuous delegation cycle.

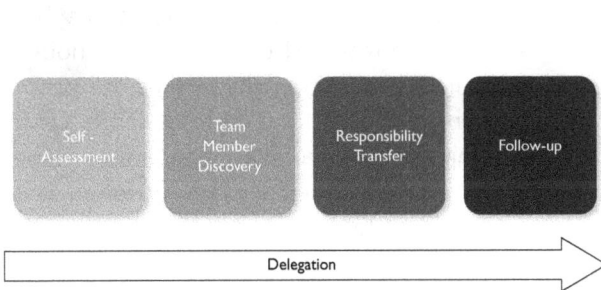

| Self-Assessment | Team Member Discovery | Responsibility Transfer | Follow-up |

Delegation

Step 1: Self-Assessment

I recommend doing up to three self-assessments. Remember, this is an investment with potential for very high returns.

1. **Read or reread "Chapter 12: E.A.S.E. Into More Effectiveness."** This chapter teaches us that before we can empower people through delegation, we must first have the discipline to prioritize our own work. The E.A.S.E. acronym can walk us through this by first eliminating what we can from our work, automating repetitive work, and simplifying processes. Only then is it fair to consider how we can delegate important outcomes because we will be less tempted to make short-term assignments and believe we are delegating.

2. **Time study**. For one full work week, in fifteen-minute increments, document where you spend your time. (You might need to round up.) For many of us, rarely do our days turn out as we plan. The purpose here is to get a glimpse into what activities are actually happening, not just what is on our calendar. An occasional time study will help us recognize time leaks (maybe we didn't realize how long those quick coffee breaks were taking), or time drains (maybe we see that we respond to email for an hour first thing in the morning, which takes our precious morning energy away from a more creative assignment.) We can then evaluate our time to see when we are the happiest and when we feel frustrated or less engaged. Having this insight will help us with the third self-assessment.

3. **Three unique, three not-unique exercise**. Using the time study and other reflections, write

down the top three responsibilities for outcomes that you feel you are uniquely qualified for AND that are fulfilling for you. Next, right down three responsibilities for outcomes you feel you are NOT uniquely qualified for and/or which are less fulfilling.

Three self-assessments may seem like a lot. Remember, they are investments in yourself and your team, with the possibility of significant returns. While I believe all three will bring the greatest impact, completing even one of them will bring great value as you take additional steps to delegate well.

Step 2: Team Discovery

This is a fun opportunity to learn about our team members. The purpose is to find out where they might be able and willing to take on more responsibilities to help them grow. Some great questions for team members are listed below. These can be asked in regular one-on-one meetings or in team meetings. They can be asked one at a time as icebreakers or all at once for deeper discussion.

1. What three to five things are you uniquely qualified for that bring you energy?
2. What three to five things, which are not necessary for you to be involved in, drain your energy?
3. What's next? What do you want to learn and/or where do you want your career to go?
4. If you could spend an entire day working on whatever you want, what would you accomplish and why?
5. What part of my job do you find most interesting/fun/satisfying/challenging? How would you like to be involved?

6. If I was promoted and we wanted you to take my place, what one area of experience/knowledge/skills would you want to focus on now so that you will feel confident in the new role?

7. In what area would you like more autonomy? What suggestions do you have to help get there?

8. In what area would you like to be known as an expert?

9. Think of a time in the last (year or month) that you were most excited to come to work. What was it that made you so excited?

10. What is the most satisfying/rewarding part of your job? How can we achieve that more often?

11. I am working on a (cool, important, complex) project. Is this something you would like to do together?

Now that we've taken time to assess ourselves, we can use this new team member information to find an opportunity to delegate.

A great example of this was when Guidant's CEO, Jeremy Ames, reflected on the fact that he was hosting every one of our weekly Monday Morning Stand-up Meetings. This meant he was gathering the information, designing the PowerPoint Presentation, then delivering the presentation each week. He realized that this wasn't something he was uniquely qualified for and that other company leaders, like me, got energy from presenting. He delegated the design of the presentation to an executive assistant who was excellent at this and really enjoyed supporting the team in this way. Then he divided up presenting opportunities amongst everyone on the leadership team.

Step 3: Responsibility Transfer

This is a model I made for myself, though I imagine other methods can achieve the same outcome. This process forces us not to short-cut the investment, instead creating deliberate and meaningful steps that will maximize team members' chances of success.

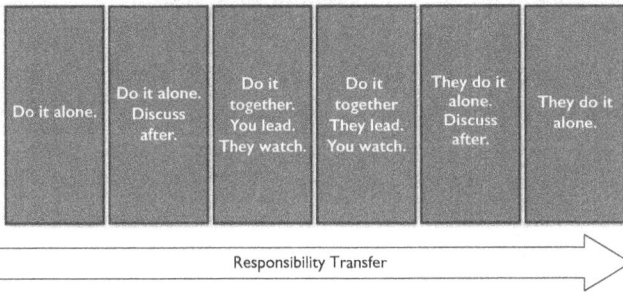

Do it alone.	Do it alone. Discuss after.	Do it together. You lead. They watch.	Do it together They lead. You watch.	They do it alone. Discuss after.	They do it alone.

Responsibility Transfer

Let's walk through a specific process together. Let's imagine that every month you write an important newsletter distributed throughout the organization. The key outcome is regular communication to keep the entire company informed. After your self-assessments and team discovery, you recognize there is someone on your team who would really enjoy doing this and will be good at it.

You're already doing it alone for now, so the next step would be to meet with this person to show them the most recent newsletter, explaining the different stages to complete it. This is also a great place to share with them:

- Thought processes and principles
- Important guardrails (like budgets or deadlines)
- Your excitement about how this will benefit them
- Expectations (desired outcome, timing, resources, anticipated challenges)

- What authority they have and where they might need to seek input
- What support is needed along the way

For the second step, you work on the next publication together. You lead while they watch. This allows them to feel safe to ask questions. This is crucial because they have the space to be thoughtful without the pressure of delivering the outcome. It is tempting to skip this step. Don't. The following month, they can take the lead while you ask questions and give appropriate feedback.

My teenage son just completed driver's education with an instructor, and knowing how frightening it must be to teach teenagers to drive, I gained a key insight when I saw that the instructor had an extra brake on his side of the car, but not a steering wheel. That's an important lesson—let's learn to guide with our words, only brake in emergencies, and resist the temptation to "take the wheel."

After these steps are completed, the individual you're delegating to should feel comfortable doing the next one on their own, because they will send it to you for feedback before it's distributed to the entire organization. Ideally, they will then be ready to go forward with all the tools, guardrails, expectations, support, and confidence to own this process.

Let's go back to the outcome: Regular communication to keep the entire company informed. Because we've delegated this outcome and taught them the current process, let's be open to new ideas. For example, if they want to test posting a weekly social media post instead or making posts twice per month on the company's intranet, let them try.

Step 4: Follow-up

Even though we reached a "do it alone" phase in Step 3, continuing to do follow-up is critical if the outcome and the person taking over are important (which they are). This is crucial for the success and confidence of that individual, which can then create more delegation opportunities.

The follow-up phase is the true sign of a great delegator and leader. Someone who takes the time to follow up on a genuine delegation responsibility is showing they care about the delegated outcome and about the person to whom they delegated.

Here are some ways to establish a good follow-up process:

1. **Have a measurement of success in place and a timeline to review it**. Perhaps it's monthly—when the target is hit, celebrate! When it's off the mark, reconnect to review the ideas and support they need to get it back on track. And still celebrate—this time, the lessons learned.

2. **Ask the team member**. See what cadence makes the most sense for meetings. They will feel supported if they control this. Some might say, let's meet monthly, or quarterly, others might tell you they'll come to you as needed. Allowing them to drive this is an important step in their autonomy. Also ask what additional support they might need at present or going forward. Maybe they want to keep building a skill and need a book recommendation or to attend a webinar, or they might want an introduction to someone in your network who is doing something similar.

3. **Add this to your one-on-one agenda, or schedule a specific meeting for checking in**.

Even if this is only reviewed quarterly because that is what they believe they need, make it a priority. Having an agenda item or a specific meeting, even for fifteen minutes, will help continue the support, confidence, and results.

Additional Tips to Delegate Like a Boss

- **"Don't work alone."**[7] This is an amazingly simple and unique way to think about delegating, outlined by John C. Maxwell in his book *The 5 Levels of Leadership*. While it's likely not practical to apply all the time, I like the spirit of it. This is a fun part of delegating where this quote and philosophy reminds me to reach out regularly to my team members to ask them to join me as I build a spreadsheet, analyze data, attend a meeting, or wrestle with a decision. Maxwell also wrote, "One of the secrets of developing leaders is to have the people you are mentoring beside you as often as possible so that they can learn how you think and act in a variety of situations. Your goal at first is for them to observe as you model leadership. But as quickly as you can, give them responsibilities that you can monitor. And as soon as they're ready, empower them to act on their own."[8]

- **"Many people refuse to delegate to other people because they feel it takes too much time and effort and they can do the job better themselves."**[9] Sound familiar? We've likely all said this at some point. That quote was from Stephen Covey. He also wrote, "Transferring responsibility to other skilled and trained people enables you to give your energies to other high-leverage activities." Remember, this is intended to be mutually beneficial, so focus on the excitement of how each of you will grow to continue fueling that investment. Let's also be open to a process or decision that might be different from how we would have done it. If you aren't familiar with Covey's "Green and Clean" story, I encourage you to check it out. It's a simple, humorous, and illustrative example of both effective and ineffective delegation with his son.

- **"Move the authority to the information, and not the other way around."**[10] This quote is from David Marquet's fantastic book, *Turn the Ship Around!* This is a real-life worst-to-first story with high stakes—a submarine crew in the U.S. Navy. The premise here changes how we think about information and decisions. Leaders often spend a lot of resources trying to get information to make decisions. Instead, we should work hard to push that decision-making down the organization where the information is already gathered (and likely best understood) in the first place.

- **"Feel grateful, not guilty."** Okay, that's a quote from me, not another world-renowned leader and author. I've heard from some leaders that an obstacle for them delegating is they feel guilty about asking someone on their team to take on more, especially if they already seem busy (and most are!) This highlights the importance of including team discovery as part of the process—you'll learn who has skills, interest, and capacity. It's an opportunity to feel grateful for team members who are already doing a lot for the team. We can also feel grateful for the opportunity to teach them the E.A.S.E. method, or otherwise evaluate their work, to lay out the top priorities and discover what will be most fulfilling for them and most impactful for the organization. Put another way, be a leader who, when you delegate an important outcome to someone with the skills and interest, works with that team member to also create the capacity to do it well and enjoy it.

- **My closet is full of shirts**. So every time I buy a new shirt, I get rid of one. I try to do the same with the assignments I take on and with the team members to whom I delegate.
- **It's okay to ask for help**. Understand that asking for help or making some assignments is acceptable. Let's just remember that this is different than delegation.

Let me wrap up with a couple of stories about delegating outcomes. The first story is, again, about my son Phoenix. When he was younger, probably seven or eight, I asked him to begin vacuuming his room since I wanted him to learn this important skill. As we looked at his room, with clothes and toys scattered all over, I was feeling pretty good about myself getting a two-for-one— him cleaning his room and vacuuming it. He was already responsible for the former; he just didn't do a great job all the time, or he procrastinated. The first time he vacuumed his room, I was excited and went to check it out with him. Sure enough, he had vacuumed. Only, he decided to vacuum around all his clothes and toys, which still littered the floor. I remember laughing and telling him that I probably wasn't clear. He said, "Why? I vacuumed my room." Indeed, he did. I just should have asked him to *clean* his room and explained that vacuuming was now a part of that cleanliness. Vacuuming a room where every item was cleared away was much more effective. Think about this story. Has this happened to you at work or at home? Where did my attempt at delegating fail? What would you have done differently?

The next story is about me leading our team through a complete remote work transition. We knew that connection was a priority and that evolving from an in-office and hybrid culture would require us to think about connection differently. This was a critical outcome. As I met with my amazing team at the time, Laura Paradis and Jason Baker, I delegated the outcome of creating connections to replace what we might have seen in our breakrooms and hallways. They blew me away with several amazing ideas, as well as the simplicity of their favorite idea to test. We were using, and still use, Microsoft Teams. They proposed we create a "Breakroom" channel and encourage people to engage here casually as they might in a physical breakroom. It was easy to test, validate the high return on the very low cost, and it is still a very active part of our culture today. Anyone can post recipes, pet pictures, bucket list achievements, travelogues, and debate who will win the Superbowl. This would have taken me weeks, and I would have over-rotated several times while Jason and Laura did this in hours. Clearly, they were skilled, had an interest, and we created the capacity for them to focus on this. The result was incredible.

Delegation is not a sign of weakness; it's a sign of a strong leader. It is one of the most important skills for us to develop in ourselves and to help other leaders develop. While the style of my eyebrows meets very few of the criteria for true delegation, it shows how difficult it can be to let go and ask for help. When the stakes are higher, it takes intentionality, the right lens, a compelling purpose, and consistent effort to delegate. The framework and tools that I've shared here can help accelerate our growth.

Here are some amazing books to sharpen this critical leadership skill:

- *Turn the Ship Around!* by David Marquet
- *Who Not How* by Dr. Benjamin Hardy and Dan Sullivan
- *The 5 Levels of Leadership* by John C. Maxwell
- *The 8th Habit* by Stephen Covey
- *One Minute Manager Meets the Monkey* by Ken Blanchard

My favorite way to remember everything here is simple: "Delegation should feel like autonomy, not abandonment." Now go delegate like a boss!

P.O.S.E. the Problem

My mom is the best. She has worked part time for many years for one reason: travel. She saves all her money to take her grown children and their spouses with her and my dad on wonderful family trips every few years.

The ten of us adults recently traveled to Roatan, Honduras, a beautiful island with amazing people, food, culture, weather, lodgings, and activities. We shared a space with my brother and his wife where our separate room's window happened to face east. The first morning, my wife and I were up very early. The sun rose around 5:00 a.m., and the sparse window coverings in our room welcomed in all that early sunlight.[1]

That night, we were tired from the wonderful activities of the day and from getting up so early. We were determined to block out the early sunlight from our window. We used bobby pins and medical tape to hang up towels and extra pillowcases. We proudly went to bed with our patchwork window coverings…which only made things worse. Not only did we wake up around 5:00 a.m. to a beautiful Honduran sunrise, we also woke up several times during the night as our contraption slowly collapsed.

On the third night, my brother offered to switch rooms. Rather than push the problem to someone else, we were invested in finding the best way to solve our problem. We asked the front desk for more blankets and sheets, fastening these new items together with shoelaces. We replaced all the missing slats in the blinds with ones from the back patio window. We thought we were finally going to have a long, good night's sleep…0 for 3. This epic creation also came tumbling down during the night.

That morning, as my wife and I were brainstorming new ideas, she was looking in the backpack that she brought on the plane. I heard her start laughing. When I looked over, she was holding two sleep masks, and asked, "Will these work?" We chuckled at the simplicity of this solution that would have revealed itself much sooner had we spent more time thinking about the problem we were trying to solve. This is why we need to invest more resources in each phase of problem-solving. Thus, predictably, I created an acronym to help me: P.O.S.E. the Problem.

Problem

Define the real problem clearly and simply. While this sounds easy, it is far more difficult than we realize. A definition must represent the real problem, going deeper than the symptoms or surface challenges. There are a lot of problem-solving tools for root-cause analysis out there like the 5 Whys, popularized by Toyota, and fishbone diagrams.[2] These and others are great options. I invite you to check out those tools if they are new to you.

A principle I've grown to love is "Fall in love with the problem, not the solution." Because we seem to be wired to want to be the one with the best answers, we use our great skills and experience to come up with solutions before we clearly define what we are trying to accomplish in the first place. Consider our early sunrise problem. The problem my wife and I were solving was "Too much light from the window," so our energy was immediately directed toward solutions for blocking the window. Had we paused to ask, "Why is light from the window a problem for us?" we would have concluded earlier on that the real problem was "We wake up too early when our eyes are exposed to sunlight." Taking a moment to figure out the actual reason the problem is a problem can help us (a) decide if it is a problem worth solving, (b) analyze the cause of the problem, and (c) explore the best options.

Using data to help define a problem can be helpful as well. For example, "Sales are trending 30 percent lower than budget, which has decreased cash reserves below $1 million."

Options

Once we have a clearly defined problem, we can effectively explore options to solve the issue. There are many great ways to generate ideas in this step. Collaborating with other people usually results in the best ideas. It's easy to take the simple problem statement to others to get their perspective or, if the problem is large enough to warrant a meeting, to set up a brainstorming session to focus on generating ideas. For brainstorming, I really like IDEO's design thinking approach that starts problem-solving with curiosity and empathy.[4] IDEO is a world-leading design company that has helped organizations design many products that we use today: shopping carts, toothbrushes, and even the first computer mouse for Apple.[5] They believe "complex problems are best solved collaboratively" and have seven rules of brainstorming:

1. Defer judgment.
2. Encourage wild ideas.
3. Build on the ideas of others.
4. Stay focused on the topic.
5. One conversation at a time.
6. Be visual.
7. Go for quantity.[6]

In my window example, when we had an inaccurate problem statement, we limited our ideas primarily to how to cover the window. While we also considered switching rooms with my brother, who is less sensitive to the light, or going to bed earlier to compensate for the early rise, we still felt that covering the window was our easiest and best solution. Once we had a better problem statement, our focus shifted from covering the window to covering our eyes. Suddenly, more and better options became available. Remember Maslow's Law of the Instrument, "If the only tool you have is a hammer, it is tempting to treat everything as if it were a nail."[7] However you choose to generate ideas, be open to many of them before falling in love with a single solution.

Solution

Once we have several options, we can evaluate which one(s) to implement. If possible, continue to leverage the perspective of those impacted and/or those you trust to provide honest feedback.

Here we might need a pros/cons list or another matrix-type tool to compare the different options based on time to implement, resources needed, expected impact, and other important factors. Considering what we have the most control or influence over can also be an important filter.

Bear in mind that doing nothing is also an option. Depending upon resources and a clear understanding of the problem and available avenues, doing nothing might be best for now.

Sleep masks for our sunlight problem became an obvious solution because they were already available to us and were the easiest and most comfortable way to block the morning light from our eyes.

Execution

Once we've decided on the best option going forward, we'll need to define who, what, when, where, and how.

Sometimes we might need to test different solutions. Figuring out the easiest or simplest way to implement something can be an invaluable lesson in itself. Be open to testing to get more information along the way or from the test itself. For example, while sleep masks became our obvious solution, not all masks are created equal. Even though the ones we had with us worked well enough for the trip, we learned that there are more comfortable options available. We investigated this before our next trip where we knew we would again have earlier sunrises.

Part of execution involves measuring the results of the solution against how we defined the original problem. After using sleep masks, all else being equal, my wife and I got sixty to ninety minutes more sleep each night, which made for a huge difference in energy, mood, and experience on our trip.

Example

To continue being a powerfully scrappy group, my team at Guidant began learning more about process improvement, problem-solving, lean principles, and system waste.

Like many organizations, we wanted to reduce turnover. The challenge with this problem is that it's often hard to understand it thoroughly enough to deliver specific and impactful solutions. Vague ideas like compensation, communication, training, and leadership may result in a lot of resources being spent on solutions that may or may not address the problem. Often, there are so many variables to consider that multiple large investments are made before the problem is truly understood or the impact is measured. Here is how we chose to P.O.S.E the Problem.

Problem. First we asked ourselves, "Why is our current turnover a problem? Where is this creating the most pain?" We realized that turnover created the most pain for existing team members who ended up carrying additional workload until we could hire and train a replacement. This additional stress often caused burnout, sometimes leading to additional turnover. So our biggest initial problem was too much time between an employee exiting and getting a replacement.

Options. With this more refined problem statement, can you see clearer ways to solve it? We could onboard better, or try to get longer resignation periods from those exiting, or hire faster, or use internal or external temporary staffing.

Solution. Our team concluded that we had the most control over the hiring process, so we decided to test some ideas to help us improve our hiring speed while maintaining quality candidates. The metrics we wanted to impact with this approach were (1) decreasing our time from exit to hire while (2) maintaining or improving our first-year retention. We set a goal to reduce our time from exit to hire from forty-seven days to thirty days or less while maintaining 90 percent first-year retention. This reasonable yet stretched target forced us to think differently and take some risks. Our solution was to define our current flow, create measurements for different parts of the hiring process, then sequentially test various ideas to meet our goals.

Execution. As our recruiter, Jason Baker was the natural owner of this problem and, with identified key partners, executor of the solution. He did a fantastic job segmenting our entire hiring process into five key areas, with steps within each area. We began tracking new metrics such as time from notice to job posting. With the foundation of a defined current process and metrics in place, the execution of different solutions happened one at a time, with a weekly check-in to identify results, new challenges, and our next best guess on the most impactful solution.

Results. In one quarter, we reduced our time from exit to hire from forty-seven days to thirty by making permanent improvements to our process. We also maintained our first-year retention numbers. A few examples here:

- We learned that we originally took up to seven business days to post a job once we knew someone was leaving or changing roles, such as being promoted. Part of the reason was that supervisors were simply waiting several days to notify us, so we asked them to let us know as soon as they knew of an upcoming transition that would require a replacement. Additionally, we set up all job descriptions, hiring plans, compensation, and other important information up front and began posting within two days.

- As I mentioned in Chapter 2, we were getting two thousand applicants for our most common role. By testing a sample size, we recognized that 50 percent of them (one thousand applicants) were outside of our compensation range and/or geographic locations for hiring. By adding and bolding our compensation range, bolding the U.S. states within our hiring footprint, and having both listed at the beginning *and* the end of the job posting, we reduced this number by around eight hundred applicants. This small effort reduced time and energy for eight hundred applicants applying for a job that wasn't a fit and saved time for the internal team that didn't need to review or process the applications.

- We partnered with Doxa Talent, an awesome outsourcing agency that supplied talent from around the world, especially the Philippines, and on their own they began hiring their most common virtual assistant roles ahead of any specific needs. That way, when we and other companies approached them with a virtual assistant opening, they already had a batch of hired and trained talent ready to interview and start within a week. That's an amazingly innovative way to approach this problem.

We hired faster and got quality candidates, so remaining team members had more support sooner. This reduced turnover. We learned that by using the P.O.S.E. the Problem method, we focused our energy and solutions on the right problem right away. Taking time for each step was critical to this success and we continue to find ways to improve our hiring process.

Conclusion

I suspect that each individual section was familiar to you from experience or prior training, which is the reason I kept the explanations short. There are many wonderful tools, books, and experts to consider for every P.O.S.E. step. While each section may seem intuitive, they aren't as instinctual as we might think. We often skip or minimize steps out of haste, overconfidence, or prematurely falling in love with a problem. Having a deliberate order, an easy-to-remember phrase, and a simple framework collectively provides a powerful structure for problem-solving.

As a coach or a business partner, this has also been useful for me in helping people escape the emotion of a problem. It helps to zoom out objectively and to thoughtfully partner together to reach a resolution.

When we P.O.S.E. the Problem correctly, we'll be able to help ourselves and those we support to understand and solve the right problems, the right way, at the right time.

Positivizing Our Communication

If you read "positivizing" in the chapter title and you're wondering if I made that word up, the answer is no. I wish I did. It's a totally real word and my second favorite verb. My first is *lightninging*, for obvious reasons—I love watching outside when it's thundering and lightninging, and it's fun to say. Positivizing is the act of making something more positive.

One Friday afternoon while I was working as a bank teller, a girl in her early twenties came into the branch and up to my space. I smiled and said, "Happy Friday!" She scowled and said, "I hate Fridays." I was so surprised to hear this that my eyes got big and my eyebrows shot up. I laughed a bit and responded, "You hate Fridays? How can you hate Fridays?" She said (and I'll remember this forever), "Because that means we are one day closer to Monday."

We need more positivity. We also need better workplaces. I see a strong correlation between the two. Looking back, I wish I had asked this girl where she worked. Chances are both she and the workplace had some opportunities to improve. Her workplace must have been so bad that she couldn't even enjoy the weekends. I've also never heard anybody say, "I can't wait to hang out with this person because they are amazing at complaining."

Our language, tone, and words matter. The way we speak can be a big part of the culture of an organization. Let me demonstrate how our communication matters.

Read this sentence out loud: "I want to be your friend."

Now, read this sentence out loud six more times to really emphasize one word at a time:

I want to be your friend.
I **WANT** to be your friend.
I want **TO** be your friend.
I want to **BE** your friend.
I want to be **YOUR** friend.
I want to be your **FRIEND**.

Notice how each time we hear that out loud, we probably extract a different meaning depending upon which word was emphasized? Having frequently heard that last one in my dating days, I can tell you each version indeed can carry different messages.

Can we agree that language is critical and being intentional about it matters? Great. Where to start? I've noticed that people usually have strong reactions to these three words: but, why, and you. Let's start there!

Eliminate Your Buts

Exercise 1: Count the number of times "but" is said. Take a day and count the number of times you say "but." Or pick a meeting with a group where there will be lots of discussion. Or do this to spice up a boring presentation and get something else out of it—research on buts.

Exercise 2: Notice the context when people use their "buts" and how you feel about the message before and after it.

Let's reflect on the reason people have a strong reaction to "buts." Here are some samples:

1. Thank you for speaking up about your idea, but we don't have time for that now.
2. That employee is smart but enthusiastic.
3. You are good at your job, but you're often late.
4. (In response to an idea)...But we don't have enough money.

When "buts" are used, people normally interpret the whole message negatively. Here are how people might perceive the four messages above.

1. Disingenuous ("but" completely neutralizes any gratitude intended with the "thank you")
2. A backhanded compliment (that may have been intended as an actual compliment)
3. Insulting
4. Contentious

Did you have these same or different reactions? Either way, it reinforces the point that people either have negative responses or different responses so we should use this awareness to communicate differently. Now that you know how often you use your "but," let's work on eliminating it.

Here are my favorite "but" replacements: "and," "so," a period, or "even though." Look at the four sample questions and think about where you would use these replacements. Here is an option:

1. Thank you for speaking up about your idea. We don't have time for that right now.
2. That employee is smart and enthusiastic.
3. Even though you are good at your job, you're often late.
4. (In response to an idea)…So we could if we find enough money.

Some people may be thinking "however" is an acceptable replacement. Someone once told me a "however" is just a "but" in a tuxedo. That made me laugh, and it's true. Let's stick to the replacement words "And," "so," a period, or "even though," Our messages will be better received, and we'll usually feel more positive ourselves when we're committed to ensuring our message will be received as intended.

P.S. Can I get credit for not caving into the temptation to say "big buts" at some point in this chapter? Thank you.

Hey You!

Starting a sentence with "You" is a truly polarizing beginning because it can be received either as powerfully positive or negative.

When giving a specific compliment, it can be sincerely received:

- You look amazing in that new sweater.
- You crushed that presentation!
- You made a huge difference for our client with your effort on the project artwork design.

It can also come across as accusatory or rude:

- You didn't send that email.
- You need to step it up to meet this deadline.

Here are the tools to add to our toolbox: "we" and point-of-view reframing. Here is how we might use those tools in the previous sentences:

- I didn't receive the email.
- We need to step it up together to meet this deadline.

By reframing our point of view, we're stating a fact from our own perspective rather than projecting what we think happened. Maybe they sent the email, and we missed it; it got snagged in a junk folder, or they accidentally typed in your email address incorrectly. Point-of-view reframing creates a positive place for this discovery to take place.

Using "we" (along with "us" and "our") creates a spirit of collective ownership and partnership. The Apple TV show *Ted Lasso* has won numerous awards and is sprinkled with amazing leadership, relationship, and life wisdom. Ted Lasso, the coach of an underachieving Premier League soccer club, says this in private to Jamie Tartt, the selfish, egotistical superstar:

"I can honestly say you are the best athlete I have ever coached. You are truly great at everything you do out there. Except for one thing. I think that you might be so sure that you're one in a million that sometimes you forget that out there you're just one of eleven. If you just figure out some way turn to that 'me' into 'us,' the sky's the limit for you."[1]

So it is for all of us.

I'm all about leverage and efficiency so, if you're looking for a place to start positivizing your communication, try this one first. When you see the shifts this one change makes, come back for the others and you will be amazed at how easy they are to implement and how this positively improves relationships and interactions.

Why Ask Why?

Like starting a sentence with "You," the question "Why" can also be very valuable in certain situations and perceived negatively in others.

When the question "Why?" is asked introspectively of ourselves or in evaluating a process, this can be a powerful tool for self-discovery and problem-solving. Toyota's concept of the 5 Whys is a great example.[2]

When a question begins with "Why" in relation to another person's thinking or behavior, this is usually perceived as accusatory. Here are a couple of common ways we might ask questions:

- Why did you do it that way?
- Why did you miss that deadline?

Here are some key replacement phrases to consider:

- Can you share/explain…
- Help me understand…
- I noticed…
- What are some of the reasons/facts…

Let's apply each of these alternatives to one of our initial questions, "Why did you miss that deadline?" Notice that it can be better received by restating from our own perspective and/or stating a neutral fact.

- I'm trying to better understand how we missed this deadline. Can you please share your perspective on this?
- I'm trying to better understand how we missed this deadline. Help me understand what you think happened.

- I noticed that we missed a deadline. What are some of the reasons you think this happened?

Sometimes we might make a wrong decision, and it's helpful to explore it, which is where I'd ask about facts: "We lost quite a bit of money on this account. What are some of the facts we relied on when we made the decision to partner with them?"

I hope you're able to reflect on the different reactions you would have if a co-worker asked you "Why did you miss that deadline?" compared to "I'm trying to better understand how we missed this deadline. Help me understand what you think happened." These shifts will help us think about how to ask questions in ways that lead to better outcomes.

A Maximum of One Negative Word per Email Communication

One of the most practical courses I took in college was my first-year Business Communications class, where we practiced responding to case study emails using a maximum of one negative word per email. Negative words include the following: *don't, not, can't, won't, aren't, sorry, unfortunately*.

This allowed me to practice positivizing my email communication. Here are a couple of examples of language evolutions:

- Don't forget about the meeting at 1:00 p.m. → Remember we have the meeting at 1:00 p.m.
- We don't take checks.→We accept cash and credit cards.

In the next email you write, see how many negative words were used. Then practice updating the language to read more positively.

Conclusion

Let me be clear. I'm not suggesting we walk around with rose-colored glasses and sugarcoat our way through life by ignoring real problems. I'm also not suggesting that if you are truly in a toxic relationship, destructive workplace culture, or dire situation, positivity alone will help. It won't. We will need to act. I am all for being honest and direct. The invitation here is to recognize that influencing others and developing strong relationships is important for our success and well-being. Any small effort to update our language can lead to major breakthroughs in how we think about others and how they respond to us.

Before sending any email, take thirty seconds to see how many "buts," "yous," "whys," and other negative words you have in it. See if you can use the tips from this section to positivize each message.

As a society, we are already good at this—we just don't realize it! The most common and most surprising place where we are usually amazing at positivizing our language: obituaries. Have you noticed that someone who was ornery is called "passionate," someone strange was "unique," and I'm certain that in my obituary I will be called "eccentric" instead of obnoxious. We often spend more time positivizing language for those who have passed than those living around us.

After meeting my Friday-hating customer, I realized that I love Mondays. It's become something that energizes me because Monday represents a clean slate and a fresh start every week. A blank canvas to paint whatever I choose. I often tell people how much I love Mondays, which I hope is infectious. Over the years, I've had a few people pull me aside and ask, "The whole Monday thing, that's a joke, right? You don't really love Mondays?" I do. And it's because I've found something to love about them. Similarly, I've found a love for improving how I develop relationships by positivizing my communication.

If you're wondering how many "buts" are in this book, I LOVE that you're thinking about that. You may see that I could have done a better job following my own ideas from this chapter. I hope we can both celebrate your increased awareness as a win and can spot places where this approach can be applied, recognizing that I am still on this journey as well. Best of luck giving these practices a shot and I hope you get the same results that I have.

Count your buts, location/situation_____

# of buts_____.

16

The 95 Percent Principle, Future Cory, and Other Prioritization Tools

I was once coaching a successful and caring executive who was amazing with their team and clients. They came to me because they wanted help to improve their time management. As we examined the problems they felt were being caused by this issue and explored solutions, we noticed a free online time management course being offered the following week. The executive registered for the course, after which we would continue creating a game plan together.

The following week, I got an email saying, "I didn't have time to attend that time management training." I'll admit I smiled at the irony then, and we've since laughed a lot about that since. The executive also noted, "Besides, it seemed like it was all about priority management and not time management." We quickly got aligned on the idea that time management *is* priority management. We planned to better understand priorities and how to make decisions with time based on those priorities.

There are some wonderful books out there on the topic of time and priority management. A few of my favorites are classics for a reason: *The 7 Habits of Highly Effective People* by Stephen Covey and *How Will You Measure Your Life* by Clayton M. Christensen.

I won't be quoting from Covey or Christensen. Instead, I will give you some additional ideas. As a Human Resources professional or a leader in any organization, the demands on our time will almost always greatly exceed our capacity, so active and skillful use of our time on the highest priorities is a capability we must understand, develop, and sustain.

Less, Better

I've taken a total of four acoustic guitar lessons in my life. The most important lesson I got from my teacher was that it's better to be able to play a few songs perfectly than to have a less-than-polished rendition of many different parts to many different songs.

We must prioritize. My philosophy is this: Do less, better. Focus on high-leverage, high-value activities, and do those well. At work, employee onboarding is that for me, as are effective one-on-one meetings. Let's give ourselves the gift of doing fewer activities so we can align (a) what we're best at with, (b) what we enjoy, and (c) what makes the biggest impact on the business and employee experience.

I asked Laura Paradis, someone who has worked with me for almost five years, if she's learned anything from me. She said this is number 1.

The 95 Percent Principle

At Ashley Manor, our CEO Keith Fletcher came into my office, and we had the following exchange:

Keith: "How much time would you need to complete some comprehensive turnover analysis?"

Me: "Probably three days."

Keith: "Can you give me fifty percent of that by tomorrow?"

Me: No.

Me (again): I'll try to get you one hundred percent by tomorrow.

As I've mentioned before, I'm a recovering perfectionist. I wanted to commit a chapter to something I created for myself that has really helped me. I call it the 95 Percent Principle.

The exact percentage is less important compared to the concept—often less than 100 percent is acceptable.

Here is an example of a hypothetical project, in this case maybe it's drafting a job description:

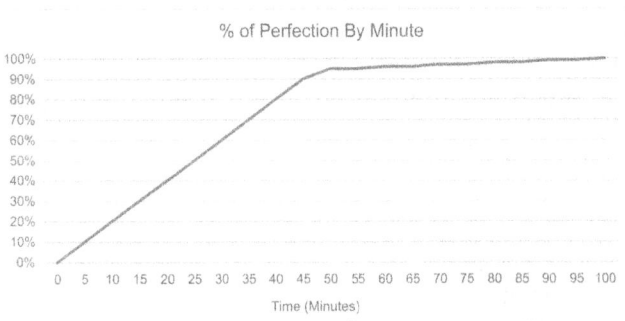

% of Perfection By Minute

Time (Minutes)

Notice that after about fifty minutes I've reached 95 percent completion or a level of acceptability. The next 5 percent might hypothetically take me another fifty minutes as I torture every word, sentence, punctuation, and formatting. Does that sound familiar? If so, then this principle is for you.

Stop at 95 percent. It's often time for a brain break, anyway. This also provides an opportunity to get someone else's perspective—I even tell them "I think I've got this 90 to 95 percent there. Now seems like a good time to get your feedback." Or, when I present data, I'll say, "This was a quick analysis, so I have about 95 percent confidence in the data. If we want 100 percent, I'll need to prioritize more time over other commitments."

Giving myself that time back allows me to have more time for another higher priority project–to 95 percent. This permission has been a gift I've been able to give myself. I'll admit it takes practice. It also takes being willing to learn when "good enough, fast," is better than 100 percent delivered later. I often have an actual feeling now, a specific moment, when I can sense that I've reached 95 percent.

Some projects will require 100 percent. Not all of them, though. With so much work to do, competing priorities, and so much administration-type work required to move the Human Resources mission forward, implementing the 95 Percent Principle can help produce more and preserve our precious energy along the way. To take a catchphrase from one of the most adult-tolerable shows my kids watched, *Yo Gabba Gabba*, "Try it! You'll like it!"[1]

Yes, When...

I have a hard time telling people "No." I want them to be happy, and I want to help them by delivering what they need from me. One of the most liberating quotes for me comes from the book *The 4 Disciplines of Execution*: "The greatest challenge you face in narrowing your goals is that it requires you to say no to a lot of good ideas."[2] The authors encourage readers to have this quote in their office, "There will always be more good ideas than there is capacity to execute."[3] Profound. Refreshing. Their bottom line: we must get good at saying no to great ideas.

Because it's hard for me to say no, I've taught myself instead to say, "Yes, when…" or "Yes, if…" Beyond just simply thinking and telling people this, which is empowering, here are a few specific ways I implement this shift in mindset.

List of Cool Ideas

Once, I didn't enjoy getting suggestions or ideas from people. This was because, to me, it felt like adding more responsibilities to my already-busy workload. People would have great ideas—highlight team members more on social media, a company service day, robust mentorship programs, and so on. If I couldn't deliver on every idea, I felt like I was letting people down. Now, though, I keep an ongoing document I call List of Cool Ideas. When I talk to people and they share thoughts and ideas with me, I tell them "I'm adding that to my List of Cool Ideas!" I explain that I get a lot of great ideas that we're not able to execute at the same time, so I keep a list of great insights like theirs to refer to when we're ready. I note who gave me the idea and when. I've had some rewarding experiences a year or two later, being able to go back to that person—one was even after they had left the organization— and reminding them of their idea and how we implemented it. Try keeping your own List of Cool Ideas as it validates every suggestion, while keeping our current commitments focused.

Another way that I make this work is by sharing our intent in advance. We have a few opportunities in our organization to intentionally seek ideas and feedback (town halls, leadership coffees, engagement surveys, strategic planning, etc.), so we tell people in advance that we want to hear from them. We share our intention to use ideas to help shape priorities—not necessarily to immediately implement every idea that we get. People appreciate the joy of sharing their ideas, especially with a clear understanding that these are brainstorming exercises where we may not be able to execute every suggestion.

Now, I really enjoy talking to people about their ideas. We have a great way to solicit and validate people's input, while keeping track of many cool ideas. And I don't have the pressure of feeling I need to implement each one.

Impact vs. Time Graph

Every time I start a new job, I draw the diagram below for my new direct manager.

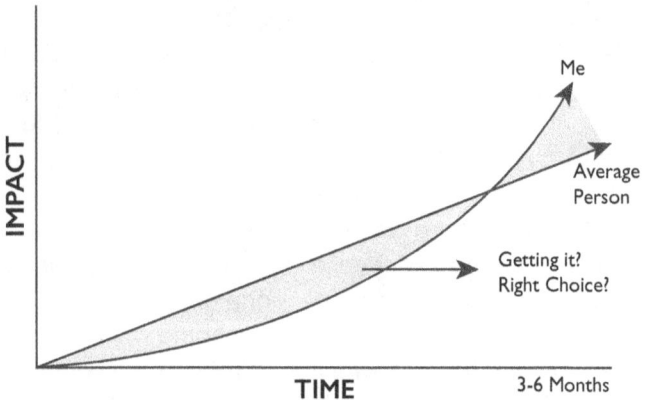

I explain that because of the way I'm wired, how I prefer to work and what I've learned from experience, I operate best if I give myself a reasonable runway before making any changes or big decisions. I prefer to learn and listen first, then make a big impact later. I acknowledge that this can be frustrating for some people. Around the three to six-month mark, they might feel like I'm behind,

I'm not getting it, or they might even be wishing they had selected someone who could have made more of an impact at this point. I share this in advance so they know that I'll accomplish their outcomes and prove their hiring decision right—with exponential impact—in time. I've been very fortunate to have leaders who have respected and embraced this. When I shared a post about this approach on LinkedIn, the CEO and co-founder who hired me at Guidant Financial, David Nilssen, wrote, "I remember you telling me to expect this and thought it was refreshing. Too many senior-level leaders feel pressure to make changes immediately. I appreciated that you wanted to listen and learn before diagnosing." If this resonates, then the leaders and companies that are right for you will welcome this perspective.

Prioritize Up

When I first started at Ashley Manor/Auburn Crest Hospice, we were mutually excited about my joining the team. As I was executing my Impact vs. Time concept mentioned before, I was taking time to talk to as many people as I could. I diligently took notes about what was working well and where we were hoping to evolve.

A few weeks into my role, we had a leadership retreat. I asked our CEO for an hour during the day. We had a good laugh when I shared with them everything I learned from them and others in the company that "Cory was going to fix," because it was three pages long.

Apparently, there were assumptions and communications from leaders that I had been brought on board to handle some very specific areas of the business and work experience. The problem was, it appeared I had only a few months to address hiring speed, compensation, training, employee recognition, timekeeping, benefits eligibility and premiums, turnover, workplace injuries, leadership development, legal compliance, and a host of other issues. There was even a rumor that I was there specifically to "fix" a single leader in the company. I joked that I better get to work! The executives and I did a selection exercise to narrow down what we felt were the top priorities for the organization and where doing one activity well in the short term would create the right foundation to positively impact most other areas.

Throughout my career, and even today, I'll have my direct supervisor come to me and ask me to complete a project or assignment. If this creates a priority and resource conflict for me, I "prioritize up" by getting them directly involved. I'll say "Yes, when we can get aligned on my current commitments. If you remember, right now I'm focused on X, Y, and Z. Will you help me understand where you see this new project in terms of priority related to my current commitments?"

This question helps me understand my leader's perspective and timing. It also allows me to focus on what the leader, and I have now agreed is the highest priority use of my time. By prioritizing up, we access the insights of smart people to help us figure out where we can make the biggest impact.

Annual and Quarterly Planning

It's crucial to do effective annual and quarterly planning for the company that cascades down to each team. This creates a priority anchor to return to at regular intervals, helping the teams to stay focused. In what will inevitably be a year of change, uncertainty, great ideas, innovations, lacking such an anchor might threaten the delivery of what has already been proactively deemed the most important outcomes.

From *The 4 Disciplines of Execution* again, "The first discipline is to focus your finest effort on the one or two goals that will make all the difference, instead of giving mediocre effort to dozens of goals." This can help in practice when ideas, projects, conference opportunities, and other resource needs arise throughout a quarter. Then we can confidently weigh this use of resources against our annual and quarterly commitments to see if they align with delivering our most important outcomes.

I know annual and quarterly planning isn't sexy or new—it just works. This planning already provides us with our answer without spending too much energy deciding in real-time, each time, where to focus resources.

Make a Promise, Keep a Promise

I lied. At the beginning of this chapter, I told you I wasn't going to quote Stephen Covey. I'm going to anyway, to make a point. In his book *Principle-Centered Leadership,* he wrote "The key to growth is to learn to make promises and to keep them."[4] Reading this, it might seem like we need to be good at, and get better at, keeping our promises. Because I would rather work with someone who made very few promises and kept them all instead of someone who made lots of promises and didn't keep them, I think our biggest opportunity is the "learn to make promises" part of the quote.

How often do you make promises you don't keep? If this is an area you feel you could improve, I encourage you to consider how to be more selective and careful about the promises you make. It will then be easier to focus on keeping those key commitments. With my broken promise in this chapter, I hope people are somewhere between slightly annoyed and mildly amused, so you can see how easy it would have been for me to not have made that promise to start with. I suspect there are many instances in our lives where we would be better off not making promises we're not sure we can keep.

If you asked Jason Fletcher, owner of Auburn Crest Hospice, where we started our multiyear journey of aligning great people around a great cause, he would tell you our mantra was "Make a promise, keep a promise." He was newly assigned as the president of the company. He asked me, as the Human Resources director of a group of companies, to become more involved in Auburn Crest Hospice. We wanted to gain trust quickly, so we decided that the fastest way to gain the trust needed to make other important changes would be to become good at both making the right promises and then being fanatically committed to delivering on them. In this manner, we could strengthen the culture, improve services, and grow the company. Our strategy worked. We won the #1 Best Places to Work in Idaho award. In addition to the award, the company doubled in size, opened new offices, acquired companies, and won multiple local awards for being the best provider of hospice services in those communities.

The prioritization tool to remember here is to be very selective of the promises we make and to whom. This can free up our time and headspace to deliver on what's most important.

Future Cory

I saved my favorite for last. One of my most-watched sitcoms of all time is *How I Met Your Mother*, which ran for nine seasons on CBS. In Season 1, Episode 8, titled "The Duel," two main characters and roommates, Ted and Marshall, are playing video games one night several weeks before Marshall would be getting married. Marshall's fiancé, Lily, had been encouraging him to have a serious talk with Ted about the fate of the apartment after the wedding. Here is their conversation during some intense video game playing:

Marshall: "So, when Lily and I get married, who's gonna get the apartment?"

Ted: "Oh, that's a tough one. You know who I think can handle a problem like that?"

Marshall: "Who?"

Ted: "Future Ted and Future Marshall"

Marshall: "Totally. Let's let those guys handle it."[5]

Incorporating this into my language with myself and my team has been a funny and effective way to prioritize. This has helped keep projects within scope, prioritize tasks, and given us permission to not over-rotate on an issue or overwork an assignment.

For example, we might be working on an important project toward the end of the day and we're tired. I might say, "Let's finish analyzing the data today, and then do you know who I think can crush sending the email about it? Tomorrow Cory. I know that guy, and I think he'll nail it."

Or we're planning an annual event where there are too many activities to fit in this year. We might say, "Let's tackle what we have this year, and let Future Cory figure out which activities to prioritize next year."

It's fun, refreshing, and it can be a powerfully effective lens to focus on what matters most right now and take things one step at a time.

Do you know who I think will crush this practice? Tomorrow You. You got this!

I will acknowledge that one of the most powerful words I've learned to say is no. This popular quote has helped me shift my perspective: "I am learning to love the sound of my feet walking away from things not meant for me."[6]

Even with these tools, I need to continually practice them. I hope one or more of these tools helps empower you to have clarity and excitement about what is most important to you and your organization, along with the energy to deliver on your commitments.

17

Anatomy of an Apology

I wrote myself up.

Seriously. I made a mistake that cost the company several thousand dollars, and I should have known better. I was embarrassed and felt bad. I filled out our written warning form and took it to my CEO's office. Keith Fletcher, the CEO, already knew about the error, so when I walked in with my write-up, he laughed and handed it back to me. It was encouraging for me when he said everything was okay, that it would be taken care of, and he knew I'd learned from it. Still, it was such a relief to acknowledge my mistake in this way.

In our roles, especially as we stretch ourselves to learn and contribute more, we will make mistakes. In addition, we are often coaching other people who have made poor choices in their behavior or productivity, and they are counting on us to help them navigate this effectively. I started using what I call the "Anatomy of an Apology"–an outline to help us and those we're coaching to approach others.

To make it easy, the Anatomy comprises four As: (1) Admit/Accept responsibility, (2) Apologize, (3) Action plan, and (4) Ask for forgiveness. Let's assume we just had a blowup with a co-worker, and we're now talking to our direct supervisor.

- Admit/Accept responsibility
    - The language here might be, "I want you to know that the argument I had with a co-worker was not acceptable. I admit that I played a major role in escalating the situation."
    - This step should also happen in a timely fashion. We need to have an active gauge to determine the right timing: fast enough so you can still be thoughtful, yet not so fast that your apology comes across as insincere. It's okay to wait until we've calmed down enough to process and be intentional, while not taking so long that the tensions are heightened.
- Apologize
    - I'm sorry for... "The negative impact my behavior had on this co-worker, the team that witnessed it, and that you had to talk to the co-worker about this situation afterward."
    - Thank you for... "Speaking to that co-worker and reaching a positive resolution when I was unable to."
- Action plan
    - Language here could be: What's next, how to prevent it in the future, repair the damage, and/or express what we've learned etc.
    - "I am planning to call the co-worker today to apologize. I want to speak to the team members to apologize as well and tell them that I've learned I get triggered when

co-workers question my work ethic. Going forward, I need to remove myself from the situation earlier."

- Ask
  - Ask for forgiveness. I like "I hope you'll forgive me." You will likely have your own preference. The key here is that we ask for it and do it sincerely. Some people will just say something like, "It won't happen again" or end with "Again, I'm sorry." I think we need to take the initiative to ask. Then we both have a shared responsibility to move forward–they will need to decide to forgive us, and we must keep the commitments we made. They might need some space and time before they forgive us. Until then, let's make sure we feel we've followed these steps and feel good that we've done what we can do to address the situation.

Here's another thought exercise: Look at the most important relationships in your life. Now think about how these deep relationships were formed:

Relationship _____

Challenges overcome together _____

Chances are these relationships are rich and meaningful, not just because you've only had easy and fun times together. You've likely supported each other through challenging times, including making mistakes and then making it right.

A mistake, followed by an effective apology, is an opportunity to grow personally and strengthen a relationship. I often remind myself of this (I make lots of mistakes), and I've found this paradigm shift for people is a powerful motivator for people to take the important step to apologize. I like to remind them that this is where stronger relationships can be formed. And, if you find yourself with the right opportunity, write yourself up. It's surprisingly liberating.

18

Your Secret Weapon

Famous authors Dale Carnegie, John C. Maxwell, and Andy Andrews in different ways all described the foundation of leadership as likeability.

In *How to Win Friends and Influence People*, a book I try to read every year, Carnegie has an entire section of six chapters/principles under the topic "How to Make People Like You."[1] While the titles of the book and section may not resonate as well today, I assure you that the principles do.

Andy Andrews, in his book *The Seven Decisions*, describes it this way: "Leadership essentially boils down to two things, your perspective or beliefs about yourself, and a quality we call 'likeability.' Likeability can be defined as the ability to build rapport so that others listen to you. We listen to the people we like."[2]

John C. Maxwell in *The 5 Levels of Leadership* writes, "Building relationships develops a foundation for effectively leading others. When people feel liked, cared for, included, valued, and trusted, they begin to work together with their leader and each other."[3]

I started my Human Resources director role with Ashley Manor/Auburn Crest Hospice on a Monday.

Pretty standard. What made it interesting was that the company already had a Human Resources director, an amazing person who had been with the company for over ten years and had successfully served in many operations roles. Company leaders wanted to bring in someone that had more direct HR experience. The existing HR director found out on Friday that I would be arriving on Monday with her job title and that I would be moving into her office. She spent Friday moving offices and likely thinking about her new role supporting the Human Resources team instead of leading it. When I came to the office on the first day, I was excited and nervous. I knew I would need to rely on her a lot in the beginning and that she might be understandably upset by the situation. I made a concerted effort to develop a relationship with her and sincerely seek her guidance. I was able to get a good start and she was a huge help. A few months later, as an icebreaker in a one-on-one meeting, I asked her how she would spend one full workday if it were completely up to her. When she told me she would spend it out in the field at our communities with our care team and residents, we worked together on a great path to return her to an operations management role where she spent many more successful years for the company. At one point, we were talking and laughing together, and she said, "You know, it is a good thing I learned to like you, because at first I wanted to get you fired."

I've worked with a few people in management positions who try to influence through their title, their expertise, or their education alone. The result: compliance and short-term commitment only. I also know many nurses and doctors who have talked to me about the toxic culture that some doctors create in the workplace because they use their status to influence. These doctors are often condescending in communicating their superiority in education and experience.

Education, experience, title, or results can all be important for success as an individual contributor to build on after likeability is achieved. Likeability leads to teamwork, which builds a positive flywheel for even more likeability, greater teamwork, and better results. Where do we start?

Here is your secret weapon: your smile.

Let's try an experiment: Who in your life has the best smile? Why do you think you remember that?

Smiles are powerful. They are memorable. They are by far the strongest weapon in our quest for likeability and good leadership. A smile radiates appreciation, enjoyment, encouragement, compassion, humor, love, kindness, and other positive emotions.

A sincere smile from another person gives me exactly what I need at that very moment. When I feel lonely, a smile helps me feel friendship. When I feel nervous, a smile helps me feel calm. When I feel discouraged, a smile can help me feel appreciated. When I've made a mistake, a smile helps me feel forgiven.

I smile genuinely as often as I can. People have shared with me the impact this has had on them. In a town hall meeting, a team member told me "When I see your smile, I feel three times brighter." People have told me that my smile has brought them comfort, enjoyment, recognition, excitement, peace, and many other feelings. By smiling, I don't intend for any specific emotion or reaction to be felt—the receiver seems to receive whatever they need in that moment.

At times, I don't feel like smiling. When I choose to smile anyway, I am usually uplifted by my own smile. A study published in Experimental Psychology concluded that smiling could improve our own mood, "When your muscles say you're happy, you're more likely to see the world around you in a positive way. We found that (smiling) stimulates the amygdala—the emotional center of the brain—which releases neurotransmitters to encourage an emotionally positive state."[4]

Critics may say that smiling too often is insincere. My response is, I can nearly always find a reason to smile. That's a choice, not deception.

When I worked at U.S. Bank as a teller, I chose to smile even if someone was really upset. My smiling conveyed that I understood they were mad at the situation or the bank and not with me personally. In my various roles, I've had to manage many difficult circumstances, conversations, and people. I've had people ask sometimes, "How can you smile when I'm upset and yelling at you?" Some were surprised that my smile completely diffused their frustration, and others were annoyed that I was smiling while they were upset. In the latter case, I really enjoy smiling even bigger and responding, "Because I like you and I genuinely enjoy helping people. I'm smiling because I have an opportunity to do the best I can to help." I don't know how that will work for others. It has worked 100 percent of the time for me.

Please do not interpret this to mean we should never be vulnerable, upset, emotional, anxious, sad, or frustrated. We need to work through those feelings authentically. Smiling can be a powerful tool to help ourselves and others to do this.

When my youngest son, Lexington, was a baby, I was very curious about smiles and their impact. When he first started smiling at a couple of months old, I could look at him and smile, and he would smile back at me. I would smile until I laughed, then he would smile and laugh. Smiles and laughter can be contagious.

Do this today (and every day):

- Find a reason to smile in a new situation.
- Smile more than you did yesterday.
- Smile at a stranger.
- Tell someone how their smile made you feel.
- Start every meeting with a smile. My profile picture in Zoom and Microsoft Teams is of me smiling big. This picture shows as a preview every time I enter a new meeting. It's a great reminder to match that smile as I enter the meeting.

In Chapter 11, about effective one-on-one meetings, I used a quote from Daniel Goleman's book *Primal Leadership* that is worth repeating here: "The fundamental task of leaders, we argue, is to prime good feeling in those they lead. That occurs when a leader creates resonance—a reservoir of positivity that frees the best in people."[5] The best way I can think of is to begin with a smile.

We can embrace our inner Buddy the Elf: "I just like to smile. Smiling's my favorite."[6]

Let's make our secret weapon not so secret anymore. Let's use our smiles to become more likable. Let's build our influence and leadership upon this likeability. Then let's use that influence to create a workplace where people are excited to make a difference for others.

SECTION 4

Sharpening Human Resources Tools

19

What a Bank Robber Taught Me about Training

In 2005, I was working as a bank teller for U.S. Bank in Boise, Idaho. I loved talking to people and helping them with their transactions.

One afternoon in June, a woman in her fifties came into the branch wearing a backpack and a fanny pack. I was intrigued—I had not seen a fanny pack since we all wore them in the 1990s! I smiled, waved her over, and told her that I would be happy to help her at my window.

She approached slowly, pulled a note from her fanny pack, and silently handed it to me. The note was written on the back of a store receipt and said, "Give me all your money and nobody gets hurt."

In rapid succession, three things happened:

- I looked at this nice woman, and thought, "For real!?"
- My life flashed before my eyes just like the movies! I immediately thought of my wife (we had only been married six weeks) and my co-workers around the bank who could be in danger.

- Then I *automatically* went into action—set the note aside, pulled my silent alarm, and gave her all the money in my drawer, including bait money. (Bait money is a set of bills only given out during a robbery because the serial numbers of the bills are recorded and saved so that the robber can be linked to the crime.)

I had just taken a large cash deposit from a restaurant, so I was handing her more bills than she expected. She first filled her fanny pack, then took two fistfuls of bills, and turned around. She walked slowly to the door, put all the money on the ground, took off her backpack, then started to scoop the bills into it.

When she had left the building, I told the other tellers to lock the door because I had just been robbed. In response to my silent alarm, U.S. Bank's security team called the branch to determine if we were being robbed. When I made my announcement, security immediately called 911, and within moments, I was on the phone with dispatch.

I had observed what direction the robber had taken. She was on foot so I thought to use the phone in our conference room with a window on the side she had left. I saw her, still walking, so I was able to tell the dispatcher exactly what she was wearing, including that awesome fanny pack, and the direction she was heading in. A bike police officer caught her just two blocks from the bank.

Even though there is much more to how this story ends, now is a good time to reflect on what this taught me about training. All the actions I took that afternoon were part of the training I received as a bank teller. I followed our protocol perfectly.

"The purpose of training is to change behavior. If people leave with just a good feeling and don't change, then the training has failed."[1] A mentor of mine, Michael

J. Glauser, told me that in 2003. I still remember it. The training provided by U.S. Bank was incredibly effective in shaping my behavior at one of the scariest moments of my life—which is when training often gets ignored.

Since that experience, I have learned that to deliver effective training there are Five Pillars (Ps) of Behavior Change:

- **Purpose:** A compelling reason to change
- **Principles:** Correct and relevant principles taught in an engaging method
- **Practice:** Role plays, case studies, activities, assessments
- **Plan:** To implement the changes and measure success
- **Partner**: To create accountability, commitments, feedback

Let's expand each category.

Purpose: The purpose statement is best completed by the person. This helps them feel genuinely connected to the outcome and motivated to achieve it. Before I started writing this book, I reached out to several author friends of mine. Each of them asked me right away, "Why do you want to write a book?" A powerful question that anchored me to a powerful purpose.

Principles: Stephen Covey in his famous book *The 7 Habits of Highly Effective People* described the seven habits as "the internalization of correct principles upon which enduring happiness and success are based."[2] Even though teaching correct principles might sound overly simple, I've attended training sessions where I saw information being imparted, but not correct principles. Someone claimed that delegation was primarily about dumping on someone else all the stuff (they used a different word) that you don't want to do. At a separate training someone claimed people are hardwired for excellence so high turnover doesn't matter as long you keep only looking for, and focusing only on, excellent people. I have a different perspective from those presenters. We should align principles with the values within our organization.

Practice: In my experience, most people do not enjoy role-playing. I am one of them. Putting me in a place where I can publicly fail is what most of my nightmares are about. Yet practice is important in developing any skill. I grew up with my dad teaching me that "Pistol" Pete Maravich would bounce a ball in the silent theatre to keep practicing his dribbling skills even while watching a movie.[3] With what we call soft skills, practice is equally important, and despite most people's aversion to it, role-playing is one of the most effective methods for learning and bolstering such skills. There are ways to make role-playing more comfortable, such as doing it in pairs or allowing people to find a different place to do it. Other powerful methods involve case studies or specific experience-shares where people apply principles directly to a situation they are facing. Assessments can also provide powerful opportunities to demonstrate knowledge.

Plan: Here is where classic goal-setting best practices come into play. Behavior change and skill adoption are best created by writing down effective goals with milestone steps and sharing them with an accountability partner. We also need to decide how we will measure success. What problem goes away, what metric will shift, what behavior will change, and how will we know?

Partner: Having an accountability partner (I will even allow the recent name conglomerate "accountabilibuddy)" is both more fun and more effective. The American Society of Training and Development found in a study that people have a 65 percent chance of achieving a goal when shared with a partner. This increased to 95 percent when there were scheduled meetings for regular follow-up.[4]

Now let's look at how U.S. Bank trained me to behave during an active robbery:

Purpose	To give myself and those in the bank the best chance to survive unharmed.
Principles	Employee and customer safety is the top priority.
	Do exactly what the bank robber asks.
	Following important steps will protect myself and the bank.
Practice	We attended a live training class in the very first week of employment. Then we read an online summary of the same concepts and took a quiz. At hire and every six months thereafter, every employee was required to watch a video depicting a robbery. We then had to answer questions and role-play the scenario with branch management. We also conducted annual drills.
Plan	Review training every six months. Knowledge was reviewed by branch auditors every year. We reviewed the training in smaller steps in regular team meetings. After a robbery, review the execution of the whole branch on security protocols.
Partner	Branch management would role-play after videos, auditors would review information annually, and a member of the bank's security team performed a post-robbery review.

This was an effective approach because I managed to do everything correctly, even while feeling that my life was in danger. I also know this can be a challenging task. Several months after my robbery, another bank in the area was robbed. In that incident, the teller tried to apprehend the robber themselves. Even though he was able to catch the robber, he lost his job. By not following the training process, he put himself and others in danger. Having been the victim of a bank robbery myself, I have mixed feelings about the decision to fire the teller. The key point is learning to build an effective training program where people behave how they are trained.

An important exercise after every training is to evaluate the effectiveness. If training went well, identify and celebrate the aspects of the 5 Ps that were done well. If they did not meet expectations, reflect on which of the 5 Ps could have been stronger to ensure a better outcome. Let's practice (see what I did there?) In the bank example where the teller broke protocol to tackle the bank robber, which of the 5 Ps do you think could be improved in their training program?

Purpose _____

Principles_____

Practice _____

Plan _____

Partner_____

Here is another example. When we wanted to invest more heavily and more effectively in supervisors at Guidant Financial, I used this same model. Here is how we designed our Leadership Development Program for the year:

Purpose	To find fulfillment in our leadership journey as we support one another and make a great positive impact with our teams. Each person completed a personal goal worksheet where they also defined their "why" for wanting to improve.

Principles	We partnered with two different external subject matter experts to train on bona fide principles for emotional resilience and effective problem-solving.
Practice	Formal training sessions included role play, case studies, and follow-up after practical application in real situations.
Plan	Each participant completed a personal goal worksheet to document where they wanted to focus, what they wanted to accomplish, key metrics to measure success, and the individual steps with timelines to achieve their goal.
Partner	Each participant already had a direct supervisor who would be part of their one-on-one meeting agenda, and they already had a Human Resources business partner to support their growth. For the program, we tested peer groups of three people to meet quarterly to share goals, practice concepts, and report on progress.

One final example demonstrates that the 5 Ps framework can be applied to any personal change or project. I once helped a co-worker lose twenty pounds. They did the hard work, of course. What I did was the following:

- Ask her why she wanted to lose weight (Purpose). She wanted to be able to water ski again with her kids.
- Ask her how she was going to accomplish the weight loss (Plan and Principles). She had a reasonable diet and exercise plan that she would follow every day (Practice).
- Create a spreadsheet that helped us track the progress to the goal with a GIF of a lady water

skiing (Partner). She had a starting weight (that she never told me) and committed to come into my office first thing every Monday to tell me how many total pounds she had lost. We recorded it on the spreadsheet together.

The 5 Ps create accountability, motivation, and the best chance for executing a plan in the midst of already very busy lives.

From an organizational culture perspective, I like to say, "People that grow, stay. Have people that stay, grow." I hope this helps us take more time to be thoughtful and intentional about the training we develop and deliver to others. I also hope that this helps us think through the improvements we want to make in our own lives and use this model to create the best chance of success.

And, yes, I absolutely used the 5 Pillars of Behavior Change to write this very book. Here is your chance to practice. Starting with a goal you've already accomplished is a great way to reflect and learn how to maximize this exercise. Think of a goal you are proud of yourself for accomplishing, then write it down along with the 5 Ps that helped you achieve it.

GOAL:	
Purpose	
Principles	
Practice	
Plan	
Partner	

Now you're ready to tackle your next goal, project, or training program!

20

My Dream Job Description

As a personal banker at U.S. Bank, my role was to open new accounts and generate new loan business. I also advised customers who had overdrawn their accounts. Fees at the time were thirty-five dollars per overdrawn transaction and seven dollars per day while overdrawn! If someone misestimated their account balance and made ten transactions before they noticed, they would suddenly see at least $350 due in fees. It was customary to waive half of the overdraft fees if the customer could make their balance current and/or apply for overdraft protection. Then at one all-district meeting, which included ten branches in the area, our district manager told us that waiving overdraft fees was losing the bank too much branch revenue so, going forward, only branch managers would be authorized to do waivers.

The next day, I had a customer consult with me about being overdrawn. We reviewed the charges and discussed ways to avoid this in the future, including online banking, alerts, and savings accounts. He did not have enough money to keep a savings account and didn't want to apply for overdraft protection because he knew his credit rating would not allow him to qualify. He just wanted me to waive all the fees. I explained that only the branch manager was authorized to do that and he was out at lunch. I told him that my manager could call him, or alternatively, he was welcome to come back, call back, or set an appointment with the manager. Instead, he left angry that I did not waive any of his fees. I felt bad about not being able to. At the same time, I also felt pleased that I had followed our new directions. Later that day, my manager pulled me aside to talk about that interaction. Somehow, this customer had contacted our district manager (the one who had given us the new overdraft fee direction), and she was upset that I hadn't provided better customer service and helped this customer with overdraft fees. I am a rule follower by nature, and I enjoy providing excellent customer service, so to give me blatantly conflicting directions and then blame me for it—well, I'll bet you can guess how I felt. Frustrated, confused, embarrassed, and angry.

A story like this could go a lot of different directions, and I'm going to steer us in the direction of my dream job descriptions. People want to succeed in their jobs. It is our responsibility as HR professionals to help bring clarity to what success looks like.

Once I accepted the job at Guidant Financial, I had the opportunity to find the next Human Resources leader to replace me at my current company. I came across Zach Townsend's profile and was quite impressed. After our conversation, he was able to persuade his current company to give him the perks that he was looking for if he moved on, so he elected to stay. Nonetheless, I was still happy that our paths had crossed. Zach and I kept in touch, and a year later, he asked me to come speak to his HR class at Boise State University, where he is a fabulous adjunct professor. He gave me a list of some awesome topics to choose from, including job descriptions. The conversation went something like this:

Me: "Yes! I want to do job descriptions!"

Zach: "Really? You heard me say training and development or recruiting, right?"

Me (laughing): "Yes, and I want to do job descriptions."

Zach (also laughing): "Okay, why did you choose job descriptions?"

Me: "Because I think they are the critical foundation for so many other cool elements in Human Resources. I want to find a compelling way to convey their importance and do it in a fun and memorable way."

Zach: "You got it. You can teach on your dream job descriptions. Good luck!"

Me (hangs up): YESSSSSSSSSSSSSSSSSS!

First, I'm going to tell you the reason I am so excited about job descriptions, then I'll share my 4 Cs for creating my dream job descriptions.

As I mentioned in the Introduction, Human Resources has many exciting and fulfilling elements: seeing people grow, advance, succeed, achieve, earn more, contribute more, innovate, create, enjoy their work, and develop meaningful relations with teammates and clients. Behind these important outcomes is an innocuous job description— like a good referee in sports, you hardly know it's there. In my experience, the better the job description is written, the easier and more sustainable the other essential elements of HR become. Additionally, job descriptions can support other key areas shown in this diagram.

Maybe you're still not on board with the crucial importance of a good job description. If that's true, I suspect it's because you know how much time it takes to create and maintain accurate job descriptions so you find it hard to see the value of investing your energy here. In this chapter, I hope to tip the cost/benefits scales in both directions: increasing your perception of their value and decreasing the time it takes to create and maintain them.

It may help if I explain what a job description is and what it is not. A job description *is* a simple, general, plain-language record of the most important elements explaining why the job exists, the top functions of the position, and supporting details about the experience needed and the work environment required to do the job. The intent is to provide enough clarity for the organization to make important decisions about the job and for the incumbent to have a general idea of the requirements and expectations.

A job description is *not* a job announcement. The difference is that a job announcement is a moment-in-time capture of the job available, which will naturally include much of the job description, along with very specific details about that particular role such as shift, part-time/full-time, location, compensation range, inspiring language around company purpose and perks, etc. A job description is also not a task list, documentation of any specific incumbent (location, part-time/full-time, name, etc.), or a place to explain benefits.

My dream job description has 4 Cs: Complete, Compact, Consistent, Compliant. Job descriptions should be written so well they need to be updated only infrequently. The 4 Cs framework helps ensure this standard.

Complete

All sections included. For me, the following are the most important elements:

- Sections
  - Job title – Let's be better here. Not everyone can be a vice president or a manager, it's our job to create more accuracy and consistency. I also once saw a job title called "Front Desk." That's furniture, not a job title.
  - Department, reports to
  - Supervisory responsibility – Yes or No
  - Fair Labor Standards Act Status: Exempt or Non-exempt
  - General summary

- o Essential functions
- o Additional duties
- o Job specifications (education, experience, knowledge, skills, abilities)
- o Work environment, physical demands
- o Legal stuff – At-will employment (if applicable), does not represent a contract, etc.
- o Employee signature
- All relevant information is included in each section.
- All acronyms spelled out.

Compact

This is giving us permission to be brief. Less is more:

- **Boring is best**. This is the job description, not the job announcement. The job description can inform much of the content of the job announcement, yet they are very different. As mentioned earlier, the job announcement can include specific details about a particular job available such as shift, part-time/full-time, location, compensation range, and inspiring language around company purpose and perks. Skip this in the job description.
- **Two pages maximum**. You can do it! It is a great and important exercise in brevity, simplicity, and priority.
- **Fragment sentences encouraged** (don't tell your high school English teacher). Example:
  - o NO: Prepare and analyze financial statements, e.g., calculating and evaluating monthly and quarterly financial reports,

forecasts, and cash projections, and present all information to CEO and other stakeholders.
- ○ YES: Prepare, analyze, and present financial statements.
- **Generic for the win**! Examples:
  - ○ Use Microsoft Excel to prepare reports → Prepare reports
  - ○ Communicate with applicants in BambooHR → Communicate with applicants in applicant tracking system (ATS)
  - ○ Host Monday Morning Stand-up → Host company meetings
- **Multitasking**. I'm on a quest to remove this language from all job descriptions. Personally, I have a hard enough time "uni-tasking," and I'm not alone. Multitasking is an illusion. Let's use job descriptions to help people really focus on what matters most and let's accept that it's unreasonable to expect multitasking.

Consistent

If we have many separate roles in our organization, this is where we can make it easiest for ourselves. Here are some keys for consistency:

- **Have a template**. This should help maintain consistency in fonts, sizes, graphics, formatting, and even some common language like the legal stuff.
- **Use best-fitting language**. There are likely many different supervisors or managers our organizations. Because every supervisor will need to perform functions of managing a team,

draft language that best describes this in your organization. Then use this standard language in every supervisor job description.

- **Start every essential function and additional duties with a verb**. Pick one verb tense and stick to it throughout the entire job description and preferably across all job descriptions. Instead of "Leads team…" and "Communicating with clients…" and "Find solutions to…" Let's pick leads, lead, or leading for the verb tense and have all other subsequent verbs match. Apply this across all job descriptions.

- **Think about why this job actually exists**, and rank the bullet points for essential functions and additional duties in priority/importance order.

- **Job titles**. Some organizations might have a director of finance and a Human Resources director. Instead, have them both start with or end with director—your choice!

- **Tone**. Again, boring is best. When required, we can make information exciting elsewhere, like in the job announcement. Whether you choose to have boring job descriptions or want them to have more personality—I once saw a job description that described the role as being "The Yoda of training"—be consistent throughout this and other job descriptions.

Compliant

- **The legal stuff**. We literally call it that in our job descriptions. You might call it something else like "disclaimer" at the end of job descriptions. Regardless, it's important to include the job status as at-will, classified, etc., and to emphasize that the job description does not create or imply a contract.

- **Other duties as assigned**. This is an important inclusion for additional work, although I've seen some controversy here. This language tries to incorporate reasonable flexibility within every job to avoid the "That's not my job" argument. For this to work, organizations must be reasonable in making requests that fall outside normal duties and compensate fairly if they are prolonged and/or represent an increase in responsibilities, such as temporarily leading a team.

- **Nothing discriminatory**. Before you roll your eyes at me, I've had to remove "young" from job descriptions when they intended it to be "new" attorneys, and I've removed "she" from job descriptions of a secretary position because that was the incumbent.

- **Very focused essential functions**. I target six to eight. Many laws are governed by essential functions, so these must be tight and reasonable. This will bring clarity to discussions around assigning light duty for a worker's compensation injury or to an interactive dialogue for disability accommodation.

- **Note the date of creation** and any dates of update (keep an archive of prior versions).

At Guidant Financial, we took some deliberate steps to specifically improve diversity and decrease unconscious bias to attract and retain more diverse individuals. I was blown away by a *Harvard Business Review* article, published in 2014, called "Why Women Don't Apply for Jobs Unless They're 100% Qualified."

Quoting an internal Hewlett Packard study, it says, "Men apply for a job when they meet only 60 percent of the qualifications, but women apply only if they meet 100 percent of them."[1] This has impacts beyond gender to include race, age, and personality types as well.

Some of the tips above are repeated and some are new, so if the only change you're looking to make (and I applaud you for it) is a focus here, then you have it all in one place.

- **Allowing experience to be equal to education everywhere possible**. Because education rates differ among different demographics, an education requirement might unnecessarily exclude talented people who have experience that equals education. Places where we made changes to allow education or equivalent experience are marketing, Human Resources, finance, 401k plan administration roles, and others.
  - ○ My dad, who started working in sales shortly after high school, was laid off in 2009 after twenty-five years in the industry. As he applied for sales jobs, he was occasionally rejected because he didn't have a bachelor's degree. These jobs didn't even require a specific degree. These companies missed hiring an amazing salesperson when they overlooked twenty-five years of successful sales and industry-specific certifications just because four of those years weren't spent obtaining a degree.
  - ○ My mom works part time at a large international company. In the middle of the Great Resignation, when staffing was

difficult due to having over ten million jobs open (the highest in United States history), her company had a policy that every employee must have a high school diploma or equivalent.[2] My mom was having a tough time keeping people on her team. She was frustrated when a woman in her fifties with fifteen years of experience with a competitor wanted to come back to the workforce and the company wouldn't hire her because she didn't have a diploma. My mom formulated an idea to eliminate this rule that wasn't serving the company anymore, then took her message as high as she could go. Shortly after, the company changed its policy. With a larger talent pool to draw from, my mom made a significant difference for the whole organization and all candidates.

- **Really short, specific, and realistic essential functions and qualifications**. If some talented people only apply if they meet 100 percent of the requirements, then let's make that list realistic and focused so we have the best chance of attracting their application.
- **Remove words like *strong*, *rock star*, *aggressive***, and other terms that might have gender-coding interpretations.
- **Eliminate jargon and spell out all acronyms**. This was mentioned earlier and has a powerful benefit for diversity. (See "Chapter 10: Death by Acronyms" for more.)

Additional tips include places to get drafts or starting points for job descriptions. Job announcements usually closely mirror job descriptions, with some additional information, and they are not copyrighted. Use job search websites to find similar job descriptions as a basis to work from. ChatGPT and other artificial intelligence tools are also becoming good at creating drafts to edit. And the U.S. Federal Government has a robust online database of job descriptions at ONETonline.org.

I'll wrap up this chapter with a few of my favorite finds on job descriptions:

- A Port Lockroy Assistant in Antarctica has these requirements: "Coordination—can you carry a big heavy box over slippery rocks and slushy snow whilst dodging penguins" and "Are you happy to not shower for up to a month, live in close proximity to three people and 2,000 smelly penguins for 5 months?"
- "For $8.50 per hour, responsible for the husbandry and care of lemurs, antelope, camels, and more. Must have bachelor's degree and at least 3-6 months of EXOTIC animal experience, work weekends and holidays, and lift a minimum of fifty pounds."

I hope these tips will give you more confidence in writing and maintaining job descriptions more easily and effectively. If this helps you make changes that encourage more people to apply for roles, makes the fun workplace elements more enjoyable, the challenging elements easier to manage, brings clarity to someone's role so they can succeed, or just gives you a longer period between updates, let's take that as win.

Visit HRYouKiddingMe.com for a sample job description template.

People Hate Surveys

People hate surveys. Okay, so *hate* might be too strong a term, though hyperbole here is useful.

I approach every survey with the assumption that people do not like to participate in them. I do what I can to mitigate the factors that cause people not to participate, not complete the whole survey, and/or not be honest.

People do not like surveys because they believe the following:

1. Nothing will change.
2. There is no immediate benefit to participating.
3. They won't ever see the results.
4. Nobody will know if I don't participate (if anonymous).
5. They are too busy, and they have higher priorities.
6. They might get in trouble for being honest. (Note: this occurs whether the survey is anonymous or not.)
7. They have survey fatigue—too many surveys, too often.

8.   They take too long.

Typically, people have a combination of the reasons listed above for refusing to take part in surveys.

So let's keep in mind why we're seeking feedback in the first place. Take an employee engagement survey. Usually, we want to get feedback from the team because we already have quantitative data (such as turnover rates), and we want to get more information directly from employees. We might be tempted to ask them too many different questions about their supervisor, pay, benefits, training, equipment, culture, etc., which usually means we're not sure what type of data is most important or most useful. Spend time really focusing on what matters most, and ask the fewest number of questions possible to find out what we need to know.

If you don't know, let me save you a lot of time and energy: communication. That's the answer every time when too many vague or poor questions are asked of clients or team members about how we can improve. Communication. And that's not particularly helpful because communication can mean something different to everybody.

I'll say it again: spend time really focusing on what matters most, and ask the fewest questions possible to achieve it. If you're interested in improving communication, ask specific questions about method, content, timing, or other important specifics so the feedback is more actionable.

I believe trends and trajectory matter more than a moment in time. Instead of perfect questions asked once, I'd rather have good questions asked over time. Even though there are a couple of questions in our quarterly survey that could be improved, I'd rather have consistency in questions that allows us to effectively measure changes being made and their impact on people's work experience over time.

Now, let's turn to participation rewards. We had some interesting results from a reward and participation correlation experiment we ran at Guidant using our quarterly engagement survey. We tried different dollar amounts and different numbers of people eligible for a randomly selected participation reward. All other variables were the same: length of time allowed to complete the survey, length of the survey, communication channels and wording, and all participants were known (not anonymous). The only substantive differences were the time of year and the reward structure.

We asked around two hundred employees each time and told them that participation would enter them into a raffle to be randomly selected for a reward. Here is the breakdown by quarter of the reward we offered and the participation it generated:

- Q1: 5 people x $100 rewards = 85 percent participation
- Q2: 10 people x $50 rewards = 76 percent participation
- Q3: 1 person x $250 reward = 70 percent participation

What is your conclusion?

Here is an additional piece of information: before this year, we only did engagement surveys annually.

Does that change your conclusion?

What I notice is a decline in participation as time went on. I believe that the dollar amounts did not impact this. (See "Chapter 22: The Reasons Bonuses Aren't Working" for additional perspective on bonuses.) While far from an academic research study, what I think happened is that, as we went from annual surveys to quarterly, survey fatigue became a real factor. Additionally, I don't believe the reward impacted participation, because we tested an anonymous survey in the following quarter to ask more sensitive questions around direct feedback for their direct supervisors. Since that survey was anonymous, we couldn't offer a reward, yet we had a 75 percent participation rate, which is about what we would expect based on prior surveys. This validates my exaggerated conclusion: people hate surveys.

Below are the best practices I've learned from conducting over one hundred different surveys for varying companies, audiences, and purposes.

Summary and Additional Tips

- **Start with a positive question, something like "What is the best part about…?"** This sets the stage for the respondents to engage with the right mindset. Even people who are frustrated should still be able to see positives about a situation and provide honest feedback in a helpful rather than just negative way. For example, when answering a question about their supervisor, someone might just say, "My boss sucks." Starting with a positive question at the beginning can help establish engagement throughout the survey, so when they get to the question about their supervisor, they might say something like this instead, "I hope my supervisor will take more time to listen to ideas I have to improve processes." Much more helpful.
- **Short surveys are generally best**. Determine and define the true purpose of the survey,

then decide on the best and fewest questions to acquire this data. Two nice safety checks are asking yourself:

- o Do any of these questions deliver overlapping or similar information? If so, which one is the best choice?
- o What will we do with this data if it is high or low? If you can't answer those questions, it might be something you're unable or unwilling to act on and might be best omitted. For example, if you're asking about employee benefits and you are unwilling to change the amount of paid time off being offered, regardless of the feedback, then it might be best to focus on topics with more flexibility.

- **Quantitative (or simple choices) vs. qualitative (open-ended; like comment boxes)**. I've learned it's best to use a combination of both. Unless there is already a culture of high participation or a lot of work upfront to communicate the type of survey, qualitative questions tend to scare people away, and quantitative questions tend to generate more responses. I've seen a lot of incomplete surveys because we've asked multiple-choice questions for the first few questions and end with several open-ended questions. Some people will complete the easy questions, then not answer the open-ended ones. I'm certain most of us have done this. Think about a satisfaction survey you've taken part in. As soon as you got away from the 1 to 5 rating scale or agree/disagree, and they asked, "Please explain why you gave that rating," you probably went, "Ughgghh!" Many people do. Let's build surveys with a balance. I try to max out at ten questions and five minutes to complete, and I also shoot for 80 percent quantitative and 20 percent qualitative.

- **Overstate the amount of time it will take to complete the survey**, just in case people take extra time. If a survey is estimated to take five minutes, I prefer to ask them to take ten minutes to participate.
- **Repeated regularly**, just not too often (I prefer quarterly for engagement surveys, for example).
- **Share summary data** with participants as soon as possible.
- **Demonstrate connections** to the survey responses and changes made.
- **Pick one or two surveys that matter most to your population** and focus on them. Limit other surveys. There are other ways to gather data like evaluating participation percentages, small random sample interviews, in-meeting polling, town halls, etc.
- **In most cases, there are trade-offs with anonymous surveys**:
  - Anonymous = lower participation, more honesty
  - Known participants = higher participation, possibly less honesty
- **Accept that the data has limitations, that it's not perfect**. Lean into this, and be transparent about that when sharing survey data.
- **Participation rewards are inconclusive**. After running some different tests with rewards, I now personally believe this is not necessary to improve participation, so we should be comfortable not offering a reward. Test what

works for your organization because rewards can be fun, just not necessary.

- **If possible, avoid using an "Other" category for responses**, since this can complicate the data analysis. Many people believe their situation is so unique that the given choices are not relevant, so they tend to over-select "Other."
- **I've found that the sweet spot to allow for survey completion is seventy-two hours**. This generally puts the survey in both the urgent and important enough categories to motivate participation. These three days must be selected carefully so they don't conflict with important deadlines, holidays, or other demanding meetings.

Not everyone hates surveys, so thank you for indulging my exaggeration. I just think it's useful to start and build from the perspective that people hate surveys. In a team meeting once, I was happy to hear an individual contributor speak up and say, "Okay guys, the annual survey is coming up in the Spring. Let's all decide together what we want from the company and share it on the survey, because they're actually listening to us and making changes based on our feedback." Total win. Surveys can be powerful when done well.

I hope these survey tips help you achieve both the participation and the quality responses you need to drive and validate important decisions in your organization.

22

The Real Reasons Bonuses Aren't Working

In our first house, my wife and I really wanted to have a small garden. Before each planting season, we first needed to pull the weeds. When my oldest son, Phoenix, was young he loved to be outside helping. He would enthusiastically help us pull weeds, and we used this to teach him to count. He also enjoyed other yardwork activities such as raking leaves, spotting wasp nests, watering pots, and planting seeds. I have fond memories and some fun pictures of us being together outside working in our yard, then enjoying the delicious food we were able to grow together.

Financial literacy is important to my wife and me, so when Phoenix was four or five years old, we thought pulling weeds would be a great way for him to start earning a little bit of money. We wanted to teach him about earning, saving, and spending. All of us were excited about him getting paid for every weed he pulled.

The first Saturday, he earned three dollars. We had a great initial conversation about money with him, so my wife and I were feeling self-congratulatory about what amazing parents we were, teaching our kids so young and so well about money.

The following Saturday, I asked Phoenix to come help me with something in the yard. He asked, "For how much money?" I explained that this time, we would just go out to spend time outside in the nice weather together. For the first time, he told me no. From that point on, way too young, he would only help me outside if I paid him. While I love how he embraced the "earning money" part of our lesson and his desire to get paid for working, I was disappointed by how quickly he forgot about how fun it was to just be spending time together and seeing the great results of our work.

I am a big believer in people receiving fair pay. On my LinkedIn page, I once posted an image of a gravestone that said "R.I.P. Unpaid Internships," with a caption saying that this is a dream of mine. I recently learned that in Europe, there are restaurants, and even entire countries like Iceland, where, instead of having servers rely on tips for income, restaurants just pay them a fair wage.[1] I would love to see more of that in the United States! Money is important in the workplace, no question. The role it plays can be misunderstood and misused, especially when it comes to bonuses.

In Simon Sinek's book *Start with Why*, Chapter 2 is titled "Carrots and Sticks." Right at the beginning of the book, he points out, "There are only two ways to influence human behavior: you can manipulate it, or you can inspire it. From business to politics, manipulations run rampant in all forms of sales and marketing. And for good reason. manipulations work."[2] He explains his use of the word *manipulation* isn't intended to be pejorative (i.e., condemning or offensive) because it's an accurate word that describes taking an action to influence someone else's behavior.

Daniel H. Pink, in his book *Drive*, cites an experiment with children and rewards for free play. "When children didn't expect a reward, receiving one had little impact on their intrinsic motivation. Only contingent rewards—if you do this, then you'll get that—had a negative effect. Why? If-then rewards require people to forfeit some of their autonomy." He also cited a study that concluded, "When institutions—families, schools, businesses, and athletic teams, for example—focus on the short-term and opt for controlling people's behavior, they do considerable long-term damage."[3]

Strong words from a couple of very popular authors. Let's examine the situations I've seen in the workplace that support their conclusions.

People Are Motivated Differently

My dad and I are excellent examples of two people who are wired differently. Not better or worse, just different. I value consistency, predictability, stability, and being fulfilled by making a positive impact. I've had discussions about bonuses for me in different roles, and my answer to my leader is always the same—I am going to work hard for you regardless of whether I have a bonus or not. I prefer to have a fair wage upfront so I can focus on the work and not the variability of my income. I'd much rather increase my base pay by some than my bonus potential by a lot. When I've shared that with people, I've had reactions ranging from complete alignment to utter incredulity.

On the other hand, my dad is the best salesperson I know. My mom jokes that he could sell sand in the desert. Remember the line from *Tommy Boy*, when David Spade (playing Richard), describes Tommy's dad as someone who could "Sell a ketchup popsicle to a woman in white gloves"? Like "Big Tommy," my dad has been selling well for decades.[4] He thrives on being 100 percent commission. Having unlimited earning potential, full accountability for his income, and achieving bonuses from sales targets is motivating for him.

Bonuses may work well for certain people and roles, while having surprisingly negative consequences for others.

Bonuses Can Incentivize the Wrong Behavior

I encourage you to seek out these great articles on this topic:

- *Harvard Business Review*: "When Economic Incentives Backfire."[5]
- Society for Human Resource Management: "When Employee Incentives Go Wrong."[6]
- *Forbes*: "Incentives Gone Wrong: How Leaders Mishandle Pay and Perks"[7]

I imagine many of us have heard of the "Cobra Effect." Or at least heard the story. Allegedly, during a time when the British government ruled India, there was an infestation of venomous cobras in Delhi. The government decided to offer a financial incentive to anyone who brought them a dead cobra. This appeared to be a great solution at first because many cobras were being killed and brought in for redemption—until it backfired. Some entrepreneurial citizens began intentionally breeding cobras to create a steady stream of new income. When the government learned of this practice, they stopped the financial incentives. The breeders released the snakes, and the problem became worse than when it started.[8]

More recently, Wells Fargo offered financial incentives for employees to sell products and open accounts. Incentives usually appear to work in the short run. Suddenly, there was a surge in new business! Soon, reports of unauthorized accounts and aggressive sales tactics jeopardized their reputation. They eventually reached a $3-billion settlement with the U.S. Attorney's Office.[9]

When I joined Guidant Financial, there was a bonus incentive program in place for our team that processes 401k plan administration tax filings to be rewarded for high production of all plans. As you can imagine, the complexity of these tax requirements varies widely, depending upon dozens of factors for each client. The more complex plans are important because they take the most time and, if not done correctly, can add exponential complexity in subsequent years. Instead of incentivizing team members to complete all filings, especially for the most complex plans, it created a system where people only focused on, and sometimes hoarded, the easiest plans. It had the exact opposite effect of what was intended.

Difficulty Tying to Something Individuals Can Control

When financial incentives are used or introduced, there is a different approach to that responsibility. People will become very focused on achieving the desired business outcome to receive the corresponding award. It can be challenging to tie an incentive directly to an outcome that an individual (or team) can control. I've seen salespeople in assisted living very upset that they can't close more sales because the operations team isn't creating a desirable product, such as how the living community looks or how the staff treats visitors. I know people who have disengaged because their incentives were tied to total business profitability and they felt they had limited or no control over the factors that drove company profitability.

When I worked as a teller at U.S. Bank, we had a bonus program based on the number of referrals we made for additional accounts, loans, or other products like online banking. When we talked to a customer about a product, we entered their name and our name into a referral system tied to our main operating system. If they opened any product within ninety days, we would be credited with a referral toward our quarterly bonus. The system seemed simple and direct enough. Well, tellers quickly learned that talking to every customer they served, even with a simple sentence like "Remember we offer home equity loans whenever you're interested," allowed them to enter this customer as a referral in the database. So imagine it's one week later. Now I'm talking to a customer at my window about their business and convince them it's time to open a business checking account. Even if I literally walk them over to the banker to open their new account right then, guess who gets credit for the referral? Not me. It could go to anyone who put that customer's name into the system for any reason. To validate the previous point above, I once noticed a teller putting in someone as a referral even though they didn't talk to the customer about a new product—they just put every single customer they helped into the referral system.

It can be frustrating having our financial fortunes depend upon other people or circumstances that are out of our control.

More Complicated than Originally Thought

Sometimes bonuses are paid out only after the achievement of a lengthy list of criteria. Or bonuses can be subject to a "clawback" if the bonus is paid first and then a disqualifying reason nullifies or decreases the amount of the bonuses.

This is because most bonus programs have many different eligibility requirements. And they probably should if they are going to anticipate all the different ways that someone might be eligible or ineligible for the bonus. Time frames, length of service, targets, extenuating circumstances, which team member earned the bonus, who is tracking the different data points, accuracy of the data, and other metrics are often part of the complexity around bonuses.

I imagine I'm in good company with others who have seen bonus programs become confusing and contentious because of their inherent complexity, along with the inability to predict all the factors that could break the system.

Difficult to Take Away

Even if a bonus program is misaligned, more expensive than anticipated, creating more problems than it's solving, challenging to track, or any other reason that justifies ending the program, it can still be problematic to stop. This is especially true for new team members who were brought on expecting bonuses and for those who regularly attain their bonus potential.

If a bonus program is stopped, people will want another opportunity to earn bonuses or will expect an increase in base pay to make up for the difference in their take-home pay. People may also leave the organization.

When we decided to remove a misaligned incentive program, we quickly lost two experienced team members who were benefiting from the unintended consequences of the program, even after we tried to make reasonable base pay adjustments.

Summary

Having complicated variable pay structures is quite common for executives of large companies. Yet, in Jim Collins's groundbreaking book *Good to Great*, he concluded, "We found no systematic pattern linking specific forms of executive compensation to the process of going from good to great. The idea that the structure of executive compensation is a key driver in corporate performance is simply not supported by the data."[10]

Okay, that felt like a lot of negativity, and I usually prefer to focus on the positives. Still, I thought it appropriate to focus first on why bonuses don't work to show just how fickle and dangerous they can be. People rarely question whether bonuses actually work, which is why they're so often seen as the solution to a wide variety of problems.

My personal feeling and practice is to be restrained in using bonuses, if only because there are usually many other ways to solve a problem, such as meaningful merit increases for exceptional performance and clear career paths to receive promotions. I focus on clarifying the desired behaviors, recognizing the effort and outcomes of these behaviors, and using inspiration instead of manipulation to drive results. This is another place where my "less is more" philosophy has served me well.

As we wrap up the chapter, I want to share another of my favorite quotes from a Daniel H. Pink presentation around motivation and the purpose money serves:

"Fact: money is a motivator at work, but in a slightly strange way. If you don't pay people enough, they won't be motivated. There is a paradox here. The best use of money as a motivator is to pay people enough to take the issue of money off the table, so they're not thinking about money, they're thinking about the work."[11]

Now, let's flip our focus to a place where we have considered the risks of bonuses and we would like to move forward and accept or try to mitigate those risks. Let's talk about some best practices:

- **See "Chapter 14: P.O.S.E. the Problem**" to clearly define the issue and introduce a bonus as one of several options to help solve the problem. Weigh the pros and cons of each option before deciding.
- **Focus on roles that already have a commission structure**. This works better for two reasons. First, variable pay is already part of the compensation structure so it's easier to add or modify a bonus. Second, people motivated by money naturally gravitate to places where they have more upside earning potential, so a bonus has a better chance of motivating them.
- **Align bonuses** with outcomes they have the most control over.
- **Be as simple and clear as possible**. Define who is eligible, how bonuses are earned, when will they be paid, if there are clawbacks or limits, where the data is coming from and who is tracking and communicating it, etc. Documenting, in addition to communicating, is imperative.
- **Introduce bonuses as tests**. I've come to see the incredible value of the concept of testing.

With it comes a lot more grace to try, succeed, fail, learn, and adapt–from others and ourselves. It gives us space to get it right, change it or remove it, with the most understanding and patience from impacted stakeholders. This also encourages people to give honest feedback on what's working and what's not.

- **Use spot bonuses instead**. This can be a small, unexpected, and powerful recognition opportunity where the team member is rewarded after doing an exceptional job on a particular project or achieving a specific outcome.

If you are (or ever have been) eligible for a bonus, ask yourself honest questions about how motivated this makes you, how much control you have over bonuses, and if there have ever been challenges with understanding eligibility criteria. This can help generate empathy as we think about how we shape compensation, motivation, and outcomes for the people we manage. Pulling weeds, killing cobras, and wildly creative people all teach us to treat compensation very carefully. And simply.

The Language of HR: Data

I love sports, and I love listening to sports broadcasts these days. Some of the data points they share are laughably specific. They might say something like, "This is the first left-handed, Texas-born quarterback over six feet tall to ever throw three touchdowns in the second quarter against a number one ranked team in November since 1971." Data is fun, and it's powerful.

I've had the privilege of having some of the most amazing Human Resources professionals on my teams for the last ten years. You could ask any one of them what's a focus area on every one of their performance reviews, and they would all likely give the same answer: Microsoft Excel. Every. Year. I once had a former team member mail me a sticker they saw at a conference that they felt I just needed to have, and sure enough, it's on my water bottle that sits beside me right now: "Data Nerd." That is a big compliment!

The language of business and business leaders is data. The best decisions come from the best data. For HR professionals to continue adding more and more value, we need to speak the language fluently. For a long time, I thought, "The *future* of HR is data" when actually, that future is already here. The most common questions I get asked as an HR leader are about either culture or data—and they are completely connected. In this chapter, I will share a few tips that I've learned about effectively using data to lead teams and support the whole organization.

The Three Metrics That Matter Most

While data is powerful, it can be overwhelming. We often feel like we have to consider many different details at the same time. In my experience, three metrics matter most. If you need a place to start simplifying what you're looking at, remember that our vehicle dashboard has only a few key gauges: speed, fuel, and temperature.

For the people in our organization, the three most important metrics are these: engagement, productivity, and retention. Those metrics encapsulate our role as HR managers: to ensure that people stay at the organization happily producing at a high level. Here's a Venn diagram for my visual friends. The intersection in the middle is our target—the ideal:

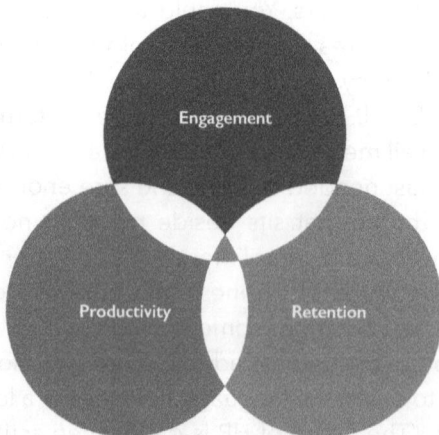

We must strive for all three, and measuring them is the first step. Let's look at what happens when we only have two:

- **Engagement and productivity**. Someone who is engaged and productive who leaves the organization goes on to benefit another company. Solution: reward them before they leave. Recognize their efforts, promote them, increase pay, provide exciting projects, etc.
- **Engagement and retention**. Someone who is engaged and stays at the organization while not being productive can be a very fun person to be around...for a while. Then peers start to notice that, as fun and engaging as they are, it's not worth picking up their slack. This is the classic case of keeping low performers that drive away high performers. Solution: coach them. Coaching might include revisiting expectations, training on needed skills, identifying and removing an obstacle, or progressive discipline.
- **Productivity and retention**: Someone who is productive and stays is a wonderful start. If they stop being engaged or enjoying doing what they're doing, this productivity likely has a short shelf life. They might become more disengaged, which could erode relationships. Solution: ask them: When are they the happiest at work, what projects are their favorite, who do they enjoy working with most, what ideas do they have that they would like to test?

Here is the Venn diagram again, now with the right action steps to take to move from two of three components to all three.

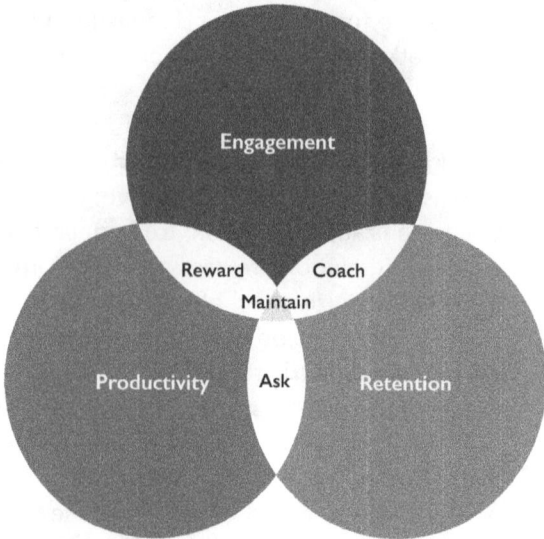

Let me add that engagement looks different to each person, which is the reason we need to ask questions so they can determine what level of engagement they're at. Does everyone have to love their job? While I hope so and work hard for that, it's not realistic. Can someone have an amazingly productive career with the same company in a job that they don't particularly like? Yes. However, it's important to realize that when we have people who meet only two of the three criteria, the HR challenges are harder. Sometimes those risks may manifest; sometimes they won't. We should acknowledge the risks and take steps to mitigate them.

As you look at the diagram, you can probably pinpoint where you're at right now. I also suspect you will be able to see where other people might be and some of the limitations if we have only one or two of the ideal elements. Hopefully, we can see the value of focusing on these three important areas, with some insight into how we can try moving from two to all three.

There is some flexibility in measuring each metric.

- Engagement can be measured by simply asking people how engaged they feel in their jobs. Other companies use a combination of questions to determine engagement. The most popular questionnaire comes from Gallup. Their questions are referred to as Q12:

  1. I know what is expected of me at work.
  2. I have the materials and equipment I need to do my work right.
  3. At work, I have the opportunity to do what I do best every day.
  4. In the last seven days, I have received recognition or praise for doing good work.
  5. My supervisor, or someone at work, seems to care about me as a person.
  6. There is someone at work who encourages my development.
  7. At work, my opinions seem to count.
  8. The mission or purpose of my company makes me feel my job is important.
  9. My associates or fellow employees are committed to doing quality work.
  10. I have a best friend at work.
  11. In the last six months, someone at work has talked to me about my progress.
  12. This last year, I have had opportunities at work to learn and grow.[1]
- Productivity can be measured enterprise-wide by revenue, sales, or labor ratio (cost of labor divided by revenue) or by department/team specific to their roles.

- Retention can be measured by total turnover or turnover by department/role. I'm personally a big fan of measuring first-year retention, whereas I don't care to spend a lot of time defining and measuring "regrettable turnover" vs. "non-regrettable" turnover. All turnover comes with a cost. There are lessons to be learned from turnover, regardless of the reason for the separation. Instead of identifying non-regrettable turnover to largely ignore it, I think we need to ask ourselves what makes this non-regrettable (usually poor behavior or performance) and find out what we can learn from the situation and what might we have done to create a better experience for the people involved.

Invest Time to Get Clean Data

A few years into being the HR director at the healthcare company, the CEO asked me what was my proudest accomplishment to that point. I had quite a few options, so he was really surprised when I answered, "Implementing job class codes." He gave me a very clear "Really?!" face, and we laughed. Now, that's a data nerd response, in case I haven't convinced you yet.

Job class codes are exactly that—a unique code for each job title. For most of our regular data analysis needs, introducing job class codes changed the near impossible to the possible-within-minutes: compensation analysis, workers' compensation audits, turnover by roles, benefits participation and eligibility breakdowns, and many others.

I regularly spend time analyzing employee data using Microsoft Excel, which has some easy-to-use filtering and pivot table tools that readily let me see where there is blank data, miscoded data, or misspellings in certain fields. These errors can impact the way data is interpreted, so this step is important to ensure clean data.

Getting and maintaining clean employee data will be different for all of us. I start by looking at our largest set of data and asking, "How confident am I in this raw data?" Explore your response to determine where you're assured and where you're not. See if you can figure out how to bridge the confidence gap with more accuracy and by putting systems in place to ensure ongoing data integrity.

Whenever I'm presenting data, I will disclose if I'm not as confident as I'd like to be about the information. For example, I might share that we asked for employee input on a topic, and we only had a 50 percent response rate. This means the data I'm sharing may not be completely representative.

I've learned several times the hard way that an "Other" category in surveys can be the death of data. As I explained in "Chapter 21: People Hate Surveys," I work hard to design survey questions and response options to avoid having an "Other" category because there will then need to be a comment box to explain their situation or perspective. If we gather lots of data and intend to summarize it, an "Other" category will require time-consuming manual effort and, often, some liberties with interpretation. This can skew the data. Artificial intelligence tools can help evaluate the written comment responses, but it's easier to avoid the need in the first place.

Use Balancing Metrics

A single metric rarely tells the whole story. Consider baseball. If someone's batting average for the year was .400, would you be impressed? That would be legendary—unless that batter played in two games, had four hits in ten at-bats, and was out with an injury the rest of the season.

Similarly, it can be enticing to focus on one data point in a process or product while ignoring other important aspects. A good example of this is speed in hiring. We could probably fill most roles within a day if we wanted to show how fast we could hire. We could finally reward the courage of the bold teenager who took the leap to apply for the chief operating officer role. Obviously, there would be major consequences in quality and performance that would make this strategy ineffective.

On the other hand, if we hold out for the "perfect candidate," it might take us a year to fill. Since no perfect candidate really exists, we need metrics to balance each other—speed and quality. For hiring speed, I like a target time to fill (from job open to signed offer letter) of six weeks or less with a balancing metric of at least 90 percent first-year retention.

Engagement, productivity, and retention can all be used collectively as balancing metrics. Described earlier in the chapter, any single metric or combination of the two is not enough to grasp the whole picture or to successfully manage a workforce. Zooming out to the whole business, we find that speed, quality, and cost are usually key metrics that balance one another effectively.

Another way to balance metrics is to use a combination of qualitative and quantitative data. I like how SurveyMonkey, a leading survey solution, describes it: "Quantitative data gets you the numbers to prove the broad general points of your research. Qualitative data brings you the details and the depth to understand their full implications."[2] This is like gathering straight turnover numbers from a Human Resources Information System (quantitative) and conducting exit interviews to determine the reasons people are leaving (qualitative).

Lead Measures and Lag Measures

Learning the difference between lead measures and lag measures was a game-changer for me. The book *The 4 Disciplines of Execution* does a great job of distinguishing them and helping to leverage each of them in the most impactful way:

"The second discipline is to apply disproportionate energy to the activities that drive your lead measures. This provides the leverage for achieving the lag measures."[3] My favorite personal example, also described in the book, is about someone who wants to lose weight. Just looking at the scale repeatedly (the lag measure) won't change somebody's weight. Acting on the lead measures (calories in and calories burned) will, over time, impact the lag measure of weight.

This is the reason that we shouldn't only rely on exit interviews or turnover data. These are lag measures that are the result of acting, or not acting, on lead measures—engagement, productivity, time between promotions, fair compensation, etc.—earlier in the employee journey. Lead measures are both predictive of the lag measure and the influenceable factors, which means we can take action to move the lag measure.

Here's how this might be used in practice: Set a lag measure goal to increase retention, and a lead measure goal for all supervisors to have quality one-on-one meetings with all their direct reports each month—something that is both predictive and influenceable. (See "Chapter 11: The Silver Bullet in Leadership*" to learn more about why I believe there is a strong correlation between direct supervisor relationships and employee experience.)

Presenting Data

Data is intended to tell a story to guide good decisions. Let's try this thought exercise: Think of a time when you saw data that was so complex or overwhelming that it actually made the conversation more confusing. What made it that way? Too much data, too many colors, different data types combined? When I think about presenting data, I think about method and rhythm. Method refers to how the data is portrayed, while rhythm is how often it is shared.

For method, charts and graphs are generally best because they can tell a great story very simply. I use a monthly scoreboard of the nine most important metrics—both lead and lag—that I use to celebrate with my team, adjust processes and priorities if needed, and to keep senior leaders informed. Having nine metrics creates a forcing function to make sure that each one is important, relevant, and displayed in a way that shows immediately if we are above a standard or below, and whether we're trending up or down. In other words, the metrics must be simple and informative. I use red and green to indicate what's on track and what's not, just enough historical data to show a trend and, in some cases, I use both percentages and absolute numbers.

Using the thought exercise earlier, I once attended a conference where a presenter shared a graph that was impossible to understand. Even on a gigantic screen, there was so much data (about twenty years' worth) along with a bar graph and a line graph using dozens of different colors. The presenter even had arrows pointing to different points of the graph using different text box explanations. I was frustrated rather than engaged. Instead of giving answers, the data created more questions. To quote the French philosopher Blaise Pascal, "I have made this longer than usual because I have not had time to make it shorter."[4] If we want to be fluent in speaking this language, brevity is important. It's easy to overwhelm people with information. It takes skill, practice, and effort to refine our data so that it meets the intended purpose of understanding problems and making important decisions. Often, less is more.

Data rhythm is something that has taken me longer to appreciate. For a data nerd like me, it can be tempting to gather and analyze all the data I can, as often as I can, to share with others. Yet many data points operate on natural rhythms. We don't need to force some data points too often or wait too long to share rapidly moving data that can be a basis for action.

In our weekly leadership team meeting at Guidant, we track our most important weekly metrics. The only metric directly related to Human Resources we review is our open role rate, which is our open roles divided by our total roles. It makes sense to focus on this every week because we know when the rate is above 5 percent, our team experiences increased stress and pain. Other traditional metrics like turnover and engagement are reported monthly and quarterly, respectively. Many people and companies would over-rotate if they saw some data too often and wouldn't make decisions fast enough if they waited too long on other metrics.

I've found the following helpful in finding the right balance:

- Gather feedback from the intended audience.
- Gather feedback from the Human Resources team on how much effort it takes to gather

certain data points and how often it is useful to gather and review the data.

- Test the process. After a few months of sharing data, ask if the data is moving fast enough to be meaningful. If no, change the cadence. Also ask, "Is the amount of time it takes to gather this data helping make important decisions to maintain or improve this metric?"
- Decide different rhythms based on the data. Here's a sample of how often I like to present data:
  - Weekly: Open role rate
  - Monthly: Time to hire, turnover, company advancements, first-year retention (rolling twelve months)
  - Quarterly: Engagement
  - Annual: Benefits participation

Like any language, it takes practice and feedback to improve effectiveness. I hope you will join me and others who see data as the present (the future is here) of the Human Resources field. We will make a significant and growing positive impact on organizational success and culture if we excel at getting good data, knowing how to analyze and interpret the information and presenting it effectively.

True to all my annual performance reviews, I'm inviting all of you to get better at Microsoft Excel this year. The cool thing about data nerds and Excel experts is that they are generally excited to share what they know. Find them and ask. You'll both be happy you did.

Be Good Consumers of Data

To be fluent in the language of data, a necessary skill is to be a good consumer of information. Here is an example of an interesting representation of data.[5] I'm curious if you see any problems with it:

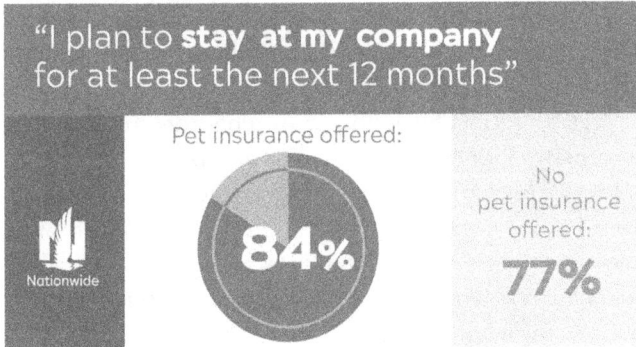

"I plan to **stay at my company** for at least the next 12 months"

Pet insurance offered: **84%**

No pet insurance offered: 77%

Nationwide

I won't dive into causation versus correlation too deeply. I just want to point out that this graphic WANTS us to believe that having pet insurance *causes* employees to want to stay at a company instead of what I suspect is true: there is merely a *correlation* between great companies that already offer great benefits and employees wanting to stay at the company for the next twelve months. Chances are, companies that offer pet insurance also have other robust employee benefits like health insurance, generous 401k matches, paid time off, and so on.

This is one of multiple ways that data can be manipulated. Let's be curious about the data that we see and ask the right questions to understand where the data came from, its intended purpose and audience, and its conclusions.

Conclusion

I have a picture to prove a very "Proud Dad" moment. When my son Phoenix was five years old, he got a ridiculous amount of Halloween candy. When he got home, he dumped out the whole sack and organized a real-life bar graph so he could see which candy he got the most. He also did this, he told me, so he could see if anyone ate one of the candies. Brilliant use of data and charts!

This might have been a chapter full of new information for some of you. For others, there might be a lot of ideas and practices you already know, in which case I hope it was validating. Either way, I hope this was the best chapter about HR data that you've ever read from a book written by a Cornell-educated nerd under six feet tall from the Boise, Idaho, area.

24

Employee "Real"ations

In my senior year of high school, I had an English teacher named Ms. Feary. She was nearing retirement, and she was also new to our school that year. I remember the look my friends and I gave one another when she introduced herself as our teacher on the first day of school. Those who know me understand I have a lot of energy. I can relate to Dani Rojas's character in *Ted Lasso* when he says, "My mother says I was born caffeinated."[1] We thought we would be able to take advantage of a new teacher to be rowdy and hilariously unmanageable. We already had high energy on that first day of school, and we were pretty disruptive in that class, immediately testing Ms. Feary's limits. We had a lot of laughs during what is normally a casual first day, anyway. After class, as the students were leaving, Ms. Feary asked if she could talk to me for a minute. My friends and others got big eyes and said, "Oooh….," thinking I was about to be in big trouble.

She waited for the rest of the students to leave and then closed the door. I thought, "Uh oh, I *am* in big trouble." After closing the door, she turned with a big smile and said, "Cory, I can tell that you are someone who likes to laugh a lot." I was totally disarmed. My only response was a confused and delayed, "Uh huh." She touched my shoulder, looked me in my eyes, still smiling, and said, "Me too! I can tell we are going to have a very fun year together." I smiled politely back, stunned. I wasn't in trouble at all—in fact, it was the exact opposite. The only difference now was that I wanted to have fun *with* her and not at her expense. This was one of the first times I remember wanting to make the class fun for the teacher as well as the students, and feeling I could do that in a respectful and not disruptive way. That day, I became her biggest advocate, and we indeed had a very fun year.

People are complicated. We bring many experiences, challenges, perspectives, biases, personalities, and preferences to the workplace. Those who can learn to work with a diverse group of people well, building each other up, are those who become the most effective leaders and HR professionals. Employee relations is a part of HR that is complex, nuanced, and where a need can arise at any moment. How team members and company leaders feel supported by HR is critical to their ongoing relationship. The HR team is only as good as its employee relations effectiveness. Sometimes, managers feel that HR people only care about the employees, while at the same time, the employees feel that HR is only there to protect the company. We must care about and balance both. Almost anyone can do the fun stuff. It's the talented and effective teams that manage the most difficult situations well.

In this chapter, I will share some observations and best practices on how we approach situations involving employee relations. I refer to it as employee "real"ations because, during crucial conversations and challenging situations, it is vital to remember that we are all human beings and we can bring a "real" human approach to our discussions and decisions. Ms. Feary is a perfect example of this. I believe my fascination with human behavior really began at that moment. She could have been irate with me and used threats, punishments, and a raised voice to keep me in line. Instead, she related to me and quickly gained my trust and support through her approach.

Employee relations are usually needed when there is a conflict, concern, or question at work. It usually encompasses a few categories: performance, behavior, leave, and policy. Employee relations might be when a team member is underperforming, or having a communication conflict with another, or needing maternity leave, or asking about the company policy for flexible schedules. Each issue might have a different frequency, urgency, and severity. Regardless of the type of conversation, here are a few best practices I've learned along the way—mostly the hard way, so you don't have to tread that path. Organizations are different, so please take the following as directional, not definitive. You might need to have discussions with other people in your organization and review company values and policies before applying these ideas.

Don't Put Out a Candle with a Fire Hose

I once worked with two different managers to handle some dress code challenges in their departments. Both managed over one hundred employees, and a few people were not following the dress code. One manager worked with me to identify these individuals and craft the right message to talk to them one-on-one. The employees appreciated the opportunity to understand the policy and being given a chance to respectfully adjust.

The other manager, despite my best coaching, wanted to send an email to the whole department instead of the one individual who was violating the dress code. This was because they didn't want to "single anyone out." Nothing changed. They sent another email to everyone. They brought it up in an all-team meeting. Still, nothing changed. Some of the best performers, and those abiding by the dress code, became frustrated and asked, "Why do we keep talking about this?" That manager finally worked with me to communicate respectfully with the person involved, who then made a change.

My wife once worked for a company that tried this approach, and an employee told her directly, "I know they are talking about me in these emails, but I'm going to keep dressing this way until they have the guts to come talk to me directly about it."

The people that we're trying to reach by putting out a candle with a fire hose—using way too much firepower—are unlikely to realize this is directed at them, or worse, they do realize and become defiant because of the indirect approach. In the meantime, 99 percent of team members who adhere to the policy have their meetings and inboxes filled up with messages meant for others.

Let's have the courage to talk to people directly and respectfully if specific individuals must change their behavior. In regards to dress codes, violations might indicate that it's time to revisit the code itself, especially since these rules are becoming more flexible in most organizations.

Same Side of the Table

My uncle was a very successful salesperson. He told me one of the secrets to his success was that he got on the same side of the table, literally, as his client. Even if invited to sit across from someone at a conference room table or across an executive desk, he would pull his chair around and sit next to them instead.

While this might work physically in some scenarios, having this mindset mentally can be just as important. I often see supervisors and HR professionals using policies, expectations, or laws as weapons–Them and the policy/law/expectation against another person. It seems like human nature to approach someone this way:

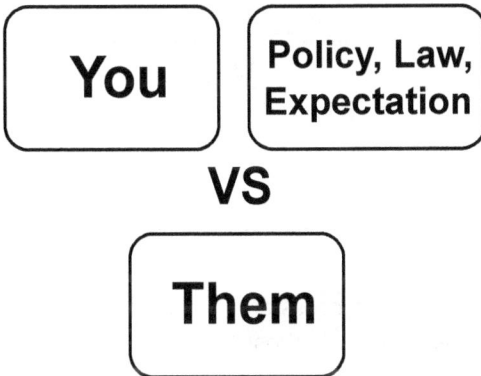

Notice that we are on the same side of the "table" as the policy, expectation, or law and it will be obvious in the language we use:

- The policy says you can't wear that kind of clothing.
- You need to figure out how to sell your quota this quarter.
- The company says that this is the most you can get paid.

- The law says you can't fire somebody for making a legit workers' compensation claim.

A more effective approach is to work with the constraints of the policy, expectation, or law and partner mentally to communicate a more collaborative approach:

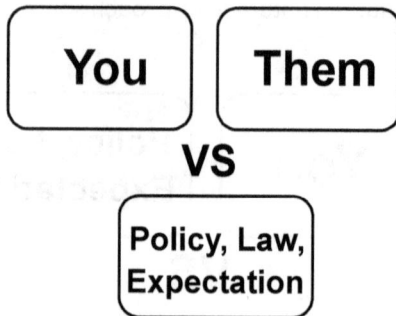

```
┌─────────┐ ┌─────────┐
│  You    │ │  Them   │
└─────────┘ └─────────┘
        VS
   ┌──────────────┐
   │ Policy, Law, │
   │ Expectation  │
   └──────────────┘
```

- We have a dress code expectation that we wear shirts with sleeves. Let's look together at how well we're doing.
- Sales quotas this quarter are XYZ. Let's look together at how we're doing in reaching that goal and discuss any additional support you need to achieve it.
- We appear to be at the maximum pay for you this year. Let's partner on what we can do this year to set you up for an increase next year, the next promotion you're hoping to get, or changes in schedule to get you more shifts or provide more flexibility for you.
- Here are the laws around workplace injuries that we are committed to follow...I know it can be hard to have someone on leave for an

extended period, so help me understand where this is causing the biggest gap and we can work together to bridge that gap until this person returns.

Another version of this is a company supervisor saying something like, "Will you let me do _____ [give someone a raise, demote somebody, use progressive discipline, send someone to a conference, etc.]?" Even though they appear to be setting up an us-versus-them scenario, this is a perfect chance to say, "Let's quickly review what the policy, expectation, or law says, and let's work together to explore what our options are within that."

Notice that we're not excusing, criticizing, or minimizing the actual policy, expectation, or law. Instead, we are using language that creates a sense that we're on the same side of the table. If you want to swing around to also sit on the same side of the table physically, go for it!

Progressive Discipline

Employee relations often involve the use of a progressive discipline process. A common progression in the United States is verbal warning, written warning, performance improvement plan, suspension, termination. There are many different philosophies and approaches. The most effective steps are those based on a genuine interest in seeing people improve and become successful in their role—with positive, timely, and direct feedback in the spirit of support.

Instead of describing each step or defending any process, let me share a few best practices for each of these steps, if your organization chooses to use them:

- **Verbal warning**. Still document. A quick follow-up email or our effective one-on-one agendas are two good options. (See "Chapter 11: The Silver Bullet in Leadership*".)
- **Written warning**. Use a template to keep these consistent. Include the policy or expectation to be met, the facts of the current situation, dates, outcomes of past discussions, and plans to support the team member's improvement.
- **Performance improvement plan**. Again, use a template to standardize this process. Common sections are the same as those in the written warning with additional sections around time frames. I recently had someone ask me, "Performance improvement plans are really joke, right? The company really intends to fire them?" If that is the case, then a big opportunity to retain a team member may be missed, or we may be wasting people's time by not moving toward an exit sooner. I said, "I hope not!" I want to set up our performance improvement plans (and other parts of progressive discipline) so that people are set up to succeed, not fail. Depending upon the role and the process cycles within, I normally use a thirty to forty-five-day time frame, and we set reasonable goals for that individual to achieve so their performance can get back on track. Any shorter may be unreasonable, and any longer may be difficult to manage and might result in unintended consequences. I once worked with an organization where the managers would set ninety-day performance improvement plans but then become really frustrated at thirty days if there wasn't progress and the employee would demand they be given the

full ninety days to try to improve. Still, there may be roles or circumstances where up to ninety days makes sense.

- **Suspension**. Some organizations use suspensions for performance or behavior-related challenges, many don't. Sometimes during an investigation involving something very serious, like discrimination or harassment, those accused or accusing might be placed on leave during this time. I prefer to call that administrative leave instead of suspension. In my experience, using suspensions well with progressive discipline has resulted in the desired performance and behavior improvements about 80 percent of the time. Suspensions are most effective when they are one to three days and in the middle of the week. That way, it's not an extended weekend, and the person has a better opportunity to really consider if this is the right role for them and, if so, whether they are willing to make the needed effort to improve behavior or performance.

- **Termination**. Even some of the best supervisors I have worked with wanted to skip reasonable progressive discipline for underperformance or moderate behavior issues and go straight to firing someone. In Chapter 11, I called this the "sock of pennies" approach. The best question to ask ourselves at termination is, "Will this person be surprised?" If the answer is yes, then there is a good chance that the steps could be improved or we may need to provide a final warning or suspension if those steps haven't been utilized yet. Let's recognize the value of the previous steps and our positive intent to help people be successful before it gets to this point. After these steps are followed, we can feel good about the efforts we've made to support the team members and they will have had multiple chances to improve. When they do, it's very rewarding.

- **Overall tips**
  - Follow defined procedure. These usually provide enough consistency to have a path and templates to follow, with the flexibility to adjust based on individual circumstances such as severity.
  - Document the important steps. Some HR professionals will say, "Document everything." Don't. That's impossible. Let's document the important performance metrics so we can equally celebrate as often as we correct, and let's document the conversations we have about behavior and performance. Emails, templates, and agendas should easily capture the dates and nature of these conversations.
  - If you have enough facts, don't wait. The problem is unlikely to resolve itself on its own. Have conversations early. Build enough trust and goodwill from compliments, effective coaching, and good leadership so this process comes much more naturally and can be resolved with verbal warnings.
  - Follow-up. Team members need to see our investment in their growth. It is our responsibility to schedule follow-up discussions to check on progress and needs.
  - The conversation about progressive discipline is best led by that person's direct supervisor. Having the next-level supervisor

or Human Resources leading these discussions, in my view, undermines the critical relationship of the direct supervisor. It completely changes the dynamic of the meeting and relationships, and people are more likely to become defensive or withdraw.

○ At every stage, provide opportunities for the team members to share their perspectives and react to the process. This should be a two-way communication that includes their active perspective.

Assume Positive Intent

A co-worker once told me an interesting story. She had gone to a branch of a large pet store chain one Sunday to get cat food. She wanted to ask a worker a question before she made her purchase. She looked everywhere and didn't see a single person in the store. She walked around the store twice, getting more and more upset at the lack of staff and attention. As she waited, she was building up the courage to tell the first employee she saw that she was a loyal customer who would switch to a competitor unless they improved their customer service. She estimates it was ten minutes before she finally saw a worker. That's a long ten minutes! Then a worker ran right up to her with a big smile and said, "Ma'am, I hope you haven't been out here long. We are actually closed right now. We don't open for another thirty minutes. Someone must have accidentally unlocked the door." She immediately relaxed, and they had a great laugh about it.

I've been told that I look like a lot of people. A woman once told me I looked like Niles from *Frasier*. Even though I died a little inside, I continually learn the life lesson that there are always two sides to every story, and I likely don't have the whole picture. I know that, in her mind, it was a compliment that came from a good place. In addition to these stories, here are more examples of misunderstandings:

- I had a friend upset with his wife for being secretive and sneaky until he showed up at his surprise birthday party.
- At work, have you ever been upset with someone who missed a meeting or was late, only to realize that you never invited them, or their dog had passed away that day, or they got delayed doing something awesome like getting bagels for the whole office?
- I once parked at the mall after it snowed during the night so there weren't visible parking lines. The snow melted while I was in the mall so when I came out several hours later, I was QUADRUPLE parked in parts of four different parking spaces. As I approached my car, a guy walking by said to his wife, "Look at this tool." I wanted to say, "He's probably an awesome guy, just misunderstood!"

When we pause to ask ourselves what some good reasons are for this event, situation, or behavior, we enter a much more empathetic frame of mind to address it. We've already allowed ourselves to see positive possibilities and to approach the situation much more objectively and compassionately.

I once had a neighbor who had a broken-down truck parked on the road right in front of our houses. One tire was off so that axle was on a wood block. The truck itself was gnarly, and I was embarrassed about having it in front of my house. I could have talked to them about my feelings, I could have filed a violation report with our homeowner's association or local police, until I gave myself a chance to assume positive intent. I assumed that they were unhappy with the situation as well and perhaps didn't have the money to fix the truck. This neighbor was a wonderful chef and sold delicious loaves of sourdough and cinnamon bread online. I went online and ordered a few loaves for our family. He was very appreciative, our family enjoyed the bread, and without ever talking about it, their truck was fixed that very weekend. Coincidence? Perhaps. What I know is, I felt good about pausing to assume positive intent and working toward a satisfactory resolution.

I've applied this to driving, and it has changed my life. Instead of being upset when someone cuts me off or merges into my lane right in front of me instead of waiting to get behind me, I tell myself they must be in a hurry. I can control leaving my house with enough time to get where I'm going, and I can be patient with everyone else around me who I cannot control. I can assume positive intent for their driving behavior. When I was commuting, I noticed a profound difference in my mood at work once I got there and when I came back home in the evening. I felt great about having waved people over with a friendly gesture instead of raising my blood pressure and car speed to make sure they didn't get ahead of me.

This applies to every aspect of our life, and I wish positive results for everyone who tries to incorporate this mentality shift.

Weaknesses Are Often Strengths

Gone Too Far

I realized something years ago that has really helped me perceive people differently: Weaknesses are often strengths gone too far. This has changed how I communicate with people when we approach challenges together. Often, these strengths embody some of their best qualities.

Here are some examples:

- Someone who is usually late: Someone who is either really casual or someone who is really ambitious
- Someone who interrupts people: Someone who loves talking to people and sharing their ideas and experiences
- Someone who considers themselves shy: Someone who is likely a really good listener

Instead of working on a personal weakness or working with someone else on a weakness, think of the exciting paradigm shift of working to reshape a strength. Someone I worked with was often late to meetings, which created disruption and inefficiencies. It's likely our instinct to say something like, "You're late all of the time and need to stop it." In a regular coaching meeting with this individual, I said something like, "I like how laid-back you are. I feel I can talk to you about anything. Do you think being so relaxed works to your disadvantage on occasion? I notice that you're sometimes late for meetings, for instance. How can we work on keeping your casual energy and being more prompt?" They responded quite positively and revealed that, because they don't want to seem tightly wound, they often have a hard time leaving a prior meeting that is running long. They then identified a few steps they could take to improve this, such as letting each meeting know at the beginning if they have a hard stop.

If this doesn't resonate with how you think about others, that's okay. Are you willing to try it on yourself? Take something you might perceive as a personal weakness, or something that others may have told you is a trait you should work on, and see if you actually have a strength that may be going too far. If this can help you give yourself some grace and approach a weakness from a new and, I think, better perspective, that's a huge win. And that might start to help all of us approach others differently.

Not So Fast, Gather Facts First

Once, after traveling with Jason Fletcher to see our teams at assisted living locations in Colorado, we were waiting for our flight home in the Denver airport when we both got a text message with this image:

Those are supposed to be meatballs. The night shift person had prepared them, and when the morning shift cooked them, these white growths emerged. A volcano of activity erupted to deal with the maggots that had somehow spoiled the meat. One person called our beef provider to tell them what happened. Another drove to the different locations in the area to collect all the remaining beef so it could be destroyed. Frantic phone calls were made to locations further out to stop using the beef until it was picked up. Somebody went to the store to buy more food.

Hours later, we got another message. A leader finally decided to talk to the night shift worker who had prepared the meatballs and was thrilled by the picture because her meatballs had turned out exactly like she'd hoped—with the rice she added to the recipe. Even though I know that it's rice, I can still hardly look at that picture. It took me a year to eat meatballs again.

Sometimes well-intentioned supervisors want to act quickly with a team member after they've heard a report from someone else. Maybe another supervisor came to them to complain about an employee who had missed the last two meetings for a project. I've had them reach out to me at this point and we have had a conversation like this:

Supervisor: "I need to give a verbal warning to somebody. Can you help me with the right way to approach it?"

Me: "For sure, tell me what happened."

Supervisor: (Explains the situation)

Me: "What was the employee's response when you asked them about it?"

Supervisor: "I didn't talk to them yet. I was waiting to be ready for progressive discipline."

Me: "Totally get that. Part of preparing for progressive discipline is gathering important facts and perspectives. It's okay to approach that team member first to bring it to their attention to see what their perspective is on the situation. You might say, "Another supervisor just mentioned to me that you weren't at the last two project meetings they've had. That's not like you, so I wanted to reach out to you first to see what your perspective is on that."

Supervisor: "Good to know that I don't have to bring discipline right away, I can ask for their side of the story first."

The ending of this story: that employee had been accidentally left off an updated meeting invitation, so they didn't know when or where the meeting was. A quick fix for a reasonable explanation. I've noticed that half the time, this is how situations turn out once we take the time to understand both sides of a story. Of course, this process will be different for an investigation of theft, harassment, discrimination, or other serious accusations.

Facts, Impacts, Goals, and Solutions (FIGS)

Boise State University has an amazing Professional and Continuing Education (PACE) program. In a leadership course I attended there, I learned from Paul Bentley a simple and helpful approach to having direct conversations that are non-judgmental. It's called FIGS: Facts, Impacts, Goals, and Solutions.[3] I've heard many different variations of this type of approach and FIGS is still my favorite.

FIGS reduces judgement and emotion, and it's as easy as it sounds. Suppose, in a meeting, someone giving a report says something that offends another person. When there's a safe place to talk about it:

- Fact(s): "In the meeting today when you said 'X'..."
- Impact: It offended Alex. Others noticed, and this changed the energy of the meeting."
- Goal: "We both want you to develop strong relationships with these team members to continue getting opportunities to work on new projects."
- Solution: "Let's talk about how we can find a solution to this and move forward. What are your thoughts on next steps?"

As I've shared this simple approach with others, I've had several people tell me this single approach has made them a significantly better leader. One even told me this made them a better spouse and parent.

The Real Magic Word: *Because*

Have you seen (or written) performance reviews that say something like, "You are an asset"?

Or had a team member in your office telling you they can't work with another person on the team because of their unreliability? Or a team member starts underperforming on their production or sales targets?

From Paul Bentley's wisdom again, the magic word in all these important scenarios is *Because*.[3] "Because" helps us move past unhelpful judgments, vague conclusions, or over-generalized compliments. Instead, it helps us be curious about what might be behind certain outcomes and behaviors.

So when we're tempted to compliment somebody in a message or a performance review with "You are an asset," let's add the word *because* afterward.

- You are an asset because….
- You believe a team member is unreliable because…
- A team member recently started underperform-ing because…

Asking and answering those questions of ourselves and others brings clarity to the situation, so we know how best to celebrate or address it.

Be Proactive

As the sayings go, an ounce of prevention is worth a pound of cure, and a stitch in time can save nine. This is true in how we engage with each other. While employee relations situations are usually reactive, most employee relations conflicts can be either avoided entirely or resolved quickly by using the following methods to proactively create clarity and develop relationships.

- Regular, effective one-on-one meetings (I know I mention this a lot!)
- Clear job expectations, clear measurement of those expectations
- Effective, ongoing training
- Clear and effective policies
- HR meetings with supervisors regularly as busi-ness partners to discuss employee develop-ment, concerns, performance, etc.

Crucial Conversations

In my opinion, the book *Crucial Conversations* should be required reading for every supervisor and HR professional. Let's review a couple of key points from the book that are helpful in Employee "Real"ations situations.

Avoid "Sucker's Choice" thinking: "We can either be honest and ruin a relationship or remain quiet and preserve the relationship."[4] Believe in, and work toward, a better third option: giving and hearing honest feedback in a manner that improves a relationship and facilitates important outcomes.

Another critical focus from *Crucial Conversations* involves mutual respect and mutual purpose. These should be the guiding principles for every supervisor and HR professional whenever we're hearing a complaint, receiving or giving direct feedback, or are otherwise engaged in a crucial conversation. Establishing mutual respect and mutual purpose up front, and making every effort to maintain it, is important to achieving the best outcome. I hope other tips in this chapter help reinforce this idea.

Tips for Managing Our Own Time, Emotions, Energy

Employee relations can be challenging and exhausting. People like me—a recovering perfectionist and someone motivated by harmony—can find these situations particularly draining. To bring our best to these situations, we must take steps to preserve and replenish our energy. Here are some tips:

- **Proactively set time limits for meetings**. I've learned the hard way (many times) that some people can talk for hours when they are upset about something. While it's important that they feel heard, it's also important to make time spent valuable. When people come into my office or send me a message to talk about something, I often will say, "I have fifteen minutes right now to meet, or if you think we'll need more time, we can set more time later today or tomorrow." This puts them in the driver's seat to decide how much time is needed. I've seen a couple of advantages here. If they elect the fifteen minutes, it's amazing how quickly we get to the root of their challenge, what they are hoping to receive from the meeting, and what the next steps should be. A meeting that may have otherwise taken forty-five minutes or longer is now both more efficient and more effective. If they want to meet later, they've often had time to cool down and come to the meeting more objectively and thoughtfully.

- **Similarly, I sometimes use parameters in my questions to help get the right information out quickly**. If trust is already established and there is alignment to explore a problem together, then using words like "brief," "summary," and "recap" can help people focus on the most important details. I might say, "I remember the situation you're referring to, so please give me a one-minute recap so we're starting on the same page for this discussion." Or, "Please give me a brief description of what happened." Mind you, this will not work well for emotionally charged situations or individuals, or if trust has to be built first. In that situation, this kind of wording will likely come across as insincere.

- **Set calendar time to focus on most important projects**. Because of these priorities already on your calendar, when employee relations situations arise, you know your commitments to work within or work around.

- **Set the bar for success at listening and being supportive rather than finding a perfect solution**. Our goal is to hear and advise, not own the problem. We don't have to have an answer right away; we can take steps to explore first. We are here to help, and we can feel good about that approachability.

- **Ask the person what they would like to see happen**. Sometimes they just want someone to listen. Sometimes they'll already have creative solutions.

- **Maintain a good work/life balance so that work can stay at work**. I like to have a physical action that I'm leaving work and becoming a father and husband. For many, this can be a commute. Because I work remotely, my signal is when I put my notebook in the drawer and close my laptop. That's my moment to leave problems at work. Exercise, sleep, reading, meditation, and being with my family are my favorite antidotes to stressful workdays.

- **Get others involved to provide insights and help share the load**. When I'm hearing a concern or complaint, I'll ask permission to discuss this with someone else to help us gather all the information and work with them to approach a solution.

The HR team is only as good as its employee relations effectiveness. Jessica Kirkendall, one of the best people I've seen manage these conversations in HR, has a wonderful attitude about working with team members. She feels valued because people trust her to discuss challenges, she sets success as listening and building trust, and chooses to enjoy the process of trying to help people find solutions and understanding. She commits to doing everything she can to help employees and accepts that they have choices they must make to help themselves be successful, without ever confusing the two.

If we embrace this important responsibility, proactively work to prevent many employee challenges, and thoughtfully discuss challenges as they arise, then we can use the tips in this chapter (and many others I'm sure you have developed) to bring a real human element to Employee "Real"ations. As we manage this critical area effectively, we'll gain the organization's trust to make big impacts elsewhere as well.

25

"Unlimited" Paid Time Off Exposed

Okay, I admit the title of this chapter is extreme. Very clickbait-y, like those videos on YouTube that are hard to resist checking out. After all, content creators use titles like this to "expose" everything from Chicken McNuggets to Tesla cars to LeBron James. I expect and hope that sharing my perspective on unlimited paid time off (PTO) will generate some thoughtful discussion and debate.

Right from the start, I want to acknowledge that no perfect system for time off exists. In one organization I worked for, we had separate accruals for vacation and sick leave. Team members frequently told us they wanted these pools combined. Some wanted more vacation time because they didn't use sick leave and they had accrued a lot of it, while others exhausted sick leave and wanted to use vacation time to be paid for the time off they needed when they were sick. The solution in their mind was to combine them. So when I worked for another organization that combined vacation and sick time into a single PTO accrual, I was really surprised to hear that some people wanted these pools separated.

There are pros and cons with each option, no matter how it's structured, what it's called, how time accrues, how accrual limits are set, how it's administered, and whether accrued time is paid out at separation. Because of this complexity, a lot of hype and misunderstanding, which is a dangerous combination, surrounds unlimited PTO. Acknowledging that any approach involves a lot of complexity, let's jump into the idea of unlimited vacation or unlimited PTO. For anyone confused by the concept, or considering it for your organization, or just wanting more information to share with other stakeholders who are pushing for this, you're in good company.

This is how different companies that have implemented unlimited PTO describe it:

1. **Netflix**: "Our vacation policy is 'take vacation,' and we actually do. Frankly, we intermix work and personal time quite a bit. Time away works differently at Netflix. We don't have a prescribed 9-to-5 workday, so we don't have prescribed time off policies for salaried employees, either. We don't set a holiday and vacation schedule, so you can observe what's important to you—including when your mind and body need a break. We believe in working smarter, not harder."[1]

2. **Roku**: "An example of trust is the Roku vacation policy. For salaried employees, we don't track vacation or have official holidays. Employees can take as much vacation as they think is appropriate, so long as they get their job done and do not block others' work or deadlines. (We simply check and give notice before taking vacation)."[2]

The benefits of unlimited PTO:

- **Recruiting**. Because of the hype, just using the phrase "unlimited PTO" can attract a lot of talented people based on their understanding and the appeal of unlimited time.
- **Extended time needed**. This can be helpful in situations where people may need more time off than usual, such as after childbirth, the death of a loved one, or medical procedures.
- **Possible cost savings**. It's my understanding that companies that offer and accrue paid time off must account for these accruals on balance sheets and retain assets to offset them. This is because many organizations also pay out unused amounts at the time of separation, so accruals act like a liability—one study estimated the costs at $272 billion for U.S. employees.[3] Note that some U.S. states require paying out accrued time at separation (and I suspect more will consider it going forward). Moving to unlimited PTO may remove separation payouts and ongoing liabilities on the balance sheet. (Please consult with legal counsel and accounting professionals if you're considering instituting unlimited PTO at your organization).
- **Culture alignment**. PTO can be culturally aligned with companies that have specific corporate values and specific industries with certain types of roles, which I'll explain later. This policy can solve problems that arise when team members feel micromanaged or companies face challenges getting the right number of days off to stay competitive.

Here are the drawbacks or hidden costs:

- It's misnamed. That should be obvious to everyone, yet we persist in calling it "unlimited" when it's not. I interviewed several people who have unlimited PTO at their companies, and my notes from one interview were powerful. They said, "It's not really unlimited. Everyone still acts as if they have about three weeks of PTO. Some take about this every year, most take less. Very few dare take more."[4]

- People may spend time working during their time off. In another interview, a friend of mine at a large, international company, whom I'll call XYZ, said, "Unlimited PTO is a running joke at our company. We call them 'XYZ vacations' because everyone just ends up working through them all, anyway."[5] A Glassdoor economic research study found that 54 percent of professionals have difficulty disconnecting during time off.[6] If the purpose of time off is to have people disconnect, re-energize, and be present in their personal lives, then this expectation or practice misses the mark.

- I was disappointed to read the following in a January 2023 BambooHR blog article titled "How Does Unlimited PTO Work? Learn the Pros and Cons": "Pro: It makes financial sense… (T)he possibility that your employees will take fewer days off (an obvious financial benefit)."[7] The opposite is true to me. If we sincerely want people to take time off because we genuinely believe in the value of personal physical and mental health, then this is not a pro, it's a major con. We shouldn't be celebrating a change where people take less time off.

- Many state and federal laws still require that time off be tracked (hence the reason I didn't add administrative savings to the benefits list above). Another person I interviewed revealed that their time was still tracked in their timekeeping system and regularly reviewed by their manager to make sure they weren't taking too much time off. If there are systems where people are still tracking time for compliance, then little time or resources are being saved.

- Notice Netflix's description above—"We don't have prescribed time off policies for *salaried* employees." (emphasis added).[8] For most companies with unlimited PTO, only salaried employees are eligible. This means that, if a company has both salary and hourly employees, there is a distinct benefits gap, and the company still must have a traditional accrual system for hourly team members. Thus, two different policies are being applied.

- See "Chapter 26: Consistency vs. Flexibility" to read more about how we are constantly trying to balance these important competing values. In this case, unlimited PTO's advertised flexibility can result in inequality and favoritism among employees. Since there are no defined limits on the amount of time off that can be taken, some employees may take advantage of the policy more frequently than others. This can create feelings of resentment and unfairness within the workforce, as certain individuals may be seen as getting preferential treatment.

- Supervisors are now in charge of managing approvals instead of a more objective system that manages much of the fairness (same accrual amounts) and approval process—do they have accrued time or not? This could villainize supervisors who don't approve as much "unlimited" time as a team member wants compared to another supervisor. A *Business Insider* article says, "Without bosses encouraging workers to take time off, the pressure to not appear greedy or lazy can keep employees from cashing in this benefit. For many workers, it can feel like borrowing time, rather than taking time you are owed."[9]

I understand these challenges apply to other PTO structures as well as unlimited PTO. I point them out there because, sometimes, people believe that unlimited PTO will solve these problems—my research tells me otherwise. In fact, there are many companies like Kickstarter that tried unlimited PTO (usually with a lot of fanfare and hype) then quietly returned to traditional accrual systems.[10]

Here is my personal perspective: unlimited PTO works for companies with only (or mostly) salaried employees doing project work where there is already a high culture of trust and flexibility. Another person I interviewed, who had experience working for two different companies that each offered unlimited PTO, said, "It worked really well at one company, and not really at the other."[11] Where it worked well, there was a small team, a high-trust culture, and well-compensated, salaried technology positions.

Other than that, I strongly believe that any problem can be solved in different ways.

- Problem: People not taking enough time off. Possible solutions: Make accruals more noticeable, speak more about this in company meetings, celebrate those who take time off, have a mechanism to track and remind people to take time off.
- Problem: Too expensive to account for and payout at separation. Possible solution: With careful consideration and legal counsel, remove paying out accrued time in states that allow this. This must be met with equally fervent efforts and sincere intent for people to actually take their time off instead of getting a big bonus for leaving the organization.
- Problem: Administration cost or time is too high. Possible solution: Simplify accruals, loosen up accrual limits or end-of-year sweeps.
- Problem: Team members want more time or it's difficult to compete for new talent with current PTO offering. Possible solution: Combine separate vacation and sick leave into a single PTO policy, increase accruals, offer floating holidays, support flexible schedules, emphasize or improve other areas of total compensation.
- Problem: Supervisors are not managing the current system well. (Note: They will not be ready to handle an unlimited PTO policy then.) Possible solutions: Training, communication, leaders setting good examples of taking time off personally, and approving the same for their team.
- Problem: Candidates and team members want more work-life balance. Possible solutions: Flexible schedules (starting, stopping, lunch), working four ten-hour days, remote work.

For companies that genuinely value the benefits of employees taking time off, regardless of the PTO structure, here are some important ways to communicate and reinforce this:

- Leaders lead by example—take time off, and approve time off for your team to support them. Do not work during PTO, and try hard not to send work to people who are on vacation. Encourage people to disable notifications on their phones while on PTO, and let's do the same. Tell people your intentions ahead of time and stick to them.
- On a regular basis (I like quarterly), remind employees and their supervisors of their accrual balances and encourage them to take time off.
- Find ways to celebrate people who took time off. With their permission, share photos from weddings, new babies, or vacations.

Unlimited PTO continues to generate buzz, especially among Gen Z and Millennials. I understand the appeal. I am a huge proponent of a positive work experience and work/life balance. I just believe we can achieve this in better and clearer ways.

At the very least, can we all agree to please stop calling it unlimited PTO? I like Flexible PTO and some companies have Minimum PTO, where employees are required to take minimum time off each year.

I've provided a lot of information, a lot of additional resources to research further, and I've tried to show that I am very much in favor of employees taking time off. I hope this chapter helped prepare you for any unlimited PTO discussions or to figure out how to maximize the effectiveness of your current program. I'll end this chapter with how I ended every English paper I wrote in high school: You decide.

26

Consistency vs. Flexibility

"Consistency and flexibility are always at odds. And when we have one, we usually want the other." My team has heard me say this mantra so often that they have it memorized, even mimicking the hand motions I make when I tap my fists together to demonstrate the tension.

We live in a business world full of competing priorities, values, and important dualities:

- Long-term vs. Short-term
- Speed vs. Quality (vs. Price)
- Urgent vs. Important
- Management vs. Leadership

It is both valuable and incredibly important to assess each of these regularly. We must strive to find the balance that works for us because focusing on just one—urgent, for example—will soon cannibalize resources from the important. In Human Resources, I've observed that we most often grapple with sustaining a healthy tension between consistency and flexibility.

Once, in our weekly leadership team meeting, Jeremy Ames, our CEO, was talking about a project where we needed to balance flexibility and consistency. Many of my peers on the call were visibly smiling and one messaged the group saying, "Music to Cory's ears."

See if you've ever experienced something like this:

Managers have flexibility to recognize the work anniversaries of their team members. This flexibility results in team members getting a different experience. Some employees receive public recognition, others receive gifts, some enjoy a team lunch, and still others receive a personal message. Then team members and leaders are concerned that these differences are negatively impacting some team members that don't get as much recognition. The company decides that consistency is important, so efforts are made to standardize anniversary recognitions. All team members now get public recognition in an all-company meeting, a thoughtful note from their supervisor, and a gift card. All managers initially agree to follow this process. Slowly, yet faster than we would like to think, some managers start providing additional public recognition for anniversaries again. They don't understand why they don't have flexibility to do what they want. They feel the standard is too rigid and suggest that managers be given more flexibility.

Sound familiar? If we're not careful, it can be a slow and challenging cycle:

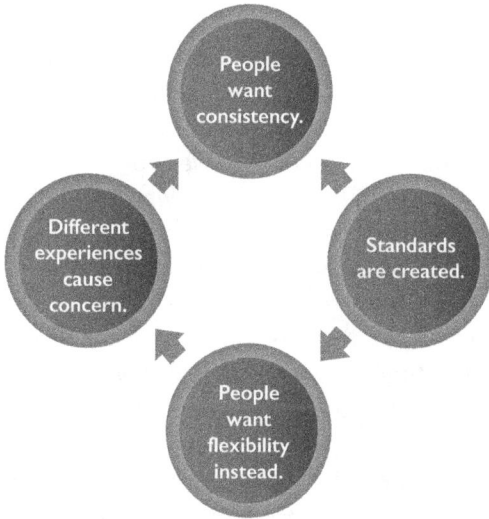

Consistency and flexibility are both important. Both can make an impact when applied in the right places. Staking a decision to one or the other when necessary, and working hard to find a place where both can exist in other situations, is an exciting core element of the HR function.

Now that you are more aware of this, I suspect you will start to see this tension in many places. That's called the Baader-Meinhof phenomenon, like when you buy a new car and then suddenly see the same model everywhere.[1] And I hope you do!

Here are some tips on how to approach this:

- Acknowledge it. The psychologist Dan Siegel designates this "Name it to tame it" when he refers to emotions.[2] It also works here. That's the reason so many people I work with now recognize this conflict before I even need to say anything.

- Determine if there are already any values, principles, or cultural norms that might help prioritize one over the other easily. If so, move forward.
- If not, find a creative way to get both. Often, we can have consistency when we think about values, expectations, resources, or outcomes while we allow some flexibility with the methods.
- Document the decision and the process (believe me—referencing the decision, reasoning, and timing is worth the effort when it gets revisited with questions down the road).

Let me share a few examples of how we've navigated the healthy tension between consistency and flexibility.

In "Chapter 11: The Silver Bullet in Leadership*", I discussed the importance of effective one-on-one meetings between every team member and their direct supervisor. I often get asked how often is best. I normally respond with my standard quote on consistency and flexibility, then highlight how we're balancing both important principles:

- Consistency: The outcome we are targeting is engaged and productive employees who stay because they feel connected. Effective one-on-ones are happening at least monthly.
- Flexibility: Length and frequency. These can be once per week for thirty minutes or once a month for forty-five minutes on any day of the week.

In "Chapter 6: Culture Is Connection," we also found a way to balance consistency and flexibility:

- Consistency: Engaged and productive employees who stay because they feel connected. We provide a menu available to every employee and some activities are required.
- Flexibility: Each team member can gauge their own needs for connection at work and participate in any optional activities they choose.

One of my favorite examples is the use of floating holidays. Companies can be consistent in offering everyone the same number of floating holidays (at Guidant, we offer two per year). People simultaneously have flexibility to use floating holidays on days that are most meaningful for them. Still, we occasionally get asked whether we can make a certain day a company holiday. The occasions most frequently brought up are Martin Luther King Jr. Day, Veteran's Day, and Hanukkah, though there are other days that are meaningful to different team members. Offering floating holidays is always a great reminder about the beauty of striking a balance between consistency and flexibility. Every team member has the same number of floating holidays per year (consistency) and can choose days that are the most important to celebrate (flexibility).

We can also learn from many examples outside of work in our local communities. I grew up skateboarding. One of the many reasons I enjoyed it was the flexibility it gave me to travel, try new tricks, and be creative skating at different locations. Many communities have struggled with inconsistencies in safety for the skateboarders and those around them, as well as the marks that skating can leave on places like curbs and benches. The genius solution: skate parks.

The first skate park was created in the 1970s in Carlsbad, California, in response to a growing skateboarding trend and a need for a safer, more controlled environment for skaters to practice and perform.[3] Before the creation of skate parks, skateboarders often had to improvise using empty swimming pools, sidewalks, and other public areas, which posed safety risks to both skaters and pedestrians. Skate parks provide a designated space for skaters to hone their skills and showcase their talents, while also reducing the likelihood of accidents and conflicts with other members of the public. Today, skate parks are a common feature in many cities and communities worldwide, providing a recreational outlet and a sense of community for skaters of all ages and skill levels.

Even though the Carlsbad skate park only lasted a few years, it sparked a worldwide solution that's an excellent example of balancing competing needs and perspectives. I have kids now who love to skateboard and scooter, and it's fun to have a place we can go together.

We must be skilled at recognizing, understanding, and navigating the healthy tension between consistency and flexibility. We must either select which is most important or be creative in finding a balance.

I'll say this one more time so you can figure out the right language for you to use, whether this or something more suitable for you: "Consistency and flexibility are always at odds. And when we have one, we usually want the other." If that was one time too many, feel free to roll your eyes. I'm used to it, and I embrace it!

SECTION 5

What's Next?

27

Traditional HR vs. HR Evolutions

I love to play the guitar. Many years ago in college, I played electric guitar in a couple of bands. Guitar strings can break from age and wear, and I had broken a couple. Standard electric guitars have six strings, so I was down to four. I was college-kid poor and couldn't afford to buy new strings.

After a first date with my future wife, I was so elated that I wanted to write a song about her and that night. I sat down with my four-string guitar and realized that I couldn't play the way I was used to. So I tuned those four remaining strings differently so that I could create all the chords and notes that I wanted to play. I wrote the music and lyrics and played it for her the next time we saw each other. We got married about nine months later.

I realized that tuning the guitar differently actually made it easier for me to play. The changes to the strings played to my strengths as a guitar player instead of me focusing on how the guitar was traditionally tuned and played. Along with that same electric guitar, I now also have two acoustic guitars–one tuned in the standard pattern, and one in my own special way. Since that night, once I could afford guitar strings again, I added and kept a fifth string on the guitar. I now proudly play many of my own songs on a five-string guitar, along with other songs I've learned to play on this unique tuning.

My guitar experience, and many other professional experiences, make me particularly bothered when I hear: "That's the way we've always done it," in response to problem or as an objection to a suggestion.

If that answer deeply bothers you as well, welcome! A large and growing group of people are helping the Human Resources profession to evolve. Just as I adapted my guitar strings to play better, we want to challenge our own assumptions and past successes to have an even more positive impact on the employee experience and business outcomes.

I want to share a few areas where I've seen success evolving from traditional HR expectations and processes.

Introductory Periods

- Traditional HR: Usually, the first ninety days for a team member in a new role. Typically, these are traditions whose purpose people no longer understand. The original reason was that ninety days was considered the time frame when a new hire could be fired for any reason, after which firing became harder.
- HR Evolution: Introductory periods are arbitrary and outdated, though they are still included in many collective bargaining agreements where this practice began. There is evidence that introductory periods can negate at-will employment by creating the perspective of guaranteed employment through the

introductory period.[1] Instead, skip this step and mindset. Treat all employee performance and feedback the same regardless of time frame. If you like having a ninety-day check-in review and/or pay increase, that can be a good practice. Understand there may be risks with a formal introductory period process because it can distort the behavior of supervisors and team members. One of the biggest risks is supervisors using this time as an excuse to not effectively manage performance.

Reference Checks

- Traditional HR: Reference checks—asking job candidates to provide names of people that they've preselected to give them glowing reviews. The intent is to help distinguish a top candidate or validate a selection decision. The responses we get from references are predictable and usually slow down the hiring process while trying to get in contact with these persons.
- HR Evolution: Instead, companies could provide the candidate with references. They're making a huge life decision, so let's help them make an informed one by *us* giving *them* references of people they can talk to that already work at the organization.

  For traditional reference checks on candidates, here are some suggestions on how to maximize their value:
  - Ask for two positive references and one from someone with whom they didn't have a great relationship at a previous job.

- If the candidate is applying for a leadership position, ask them to provide at least one reference from someone who reported to them.
- Instead of asking for references, ask the candidate directly, "What will your references tell us about (fill in the blank)?" This could be attendance, getting along with others, technical skills, etc. This puts the candidate in a more objective place to answer these questions honestly.
- It's hard to get "weaknesses" type answers from references besides cliches like they work too hard and care too much. I like to ask about the *next* role they might be promoted to. "If we hired Sara for this role and put her on path to promote her to lead the team, where should we focus her training to get her there fastest?"
- Or skip them altogether and enjoy the faster hiring time.

Cover Letters

- Traditional HR: Can provide an extra step for candidates to "prove" they are serious about this role, which may eliminate unqualified or uncommitted candidates. Cover letters are also supposed to be a place where someone can bring their résumé to life by showing a little more personality, demonstrate writing skills, and connecting the résumé details with the job requirements.

- HR Evolution: Skip cover letters. I've asked a lot of recruiters if they read them, and most of them admit almost never. They are becoming more obsolete with artificial intelligence (AI) tools doing a lot of people's writing these days.

  Plus, applicant tracking systems (some with the use of AI) are much better at filtering candidates, so we don't need to create an additional burden on them just for filtering purposes.

I've found that the simpler the hiring process, the more diverse the candidates (sex, race, gender, age, experience, personality, education, etc.) the role will attract.

Unpaid Internships

- Traditional HR: As of this writing and based on my understanding of current federal laws, nonprofit organizations, including governments, have more flexibility to offer unpaid internships. For-profit companies, according to the Department of Labor, must meet seven criteria to consider an internship as unpaid.[2]
- HR Evolution: In my exploration of this topic, I've heard justifications for unpaid internships everywhere from, "Hey, it's free labor" to "We can't afford to pay interns" to "We are XYZ company, and we are so amazing that they should feel grateful to just learn from us without getting paid" or "They're getting paid in experience."

I once asked an Idaho Department of Labor employee with ten years of experience if he had ever seen a for-profit company meet all the requirements to offer unpaid internships. He scoffed before simply saying "No."

I am the beneficiary of a paid internship at Ada County that launched my HR career. This allowed me to make enough money to focus on school and work at the same time. I hope we can bring this experience to more people. Internships can be wonderful learning experiences. Let's pay people a reasonable amount to allow them to embrace the experience without worrying about finances. If we really want people to learn, they'll do it better when financial stress is decreased.

While there may be narrow opportunities for volunteers or unpaid interns in nonprofit and government agencies, such as teaching a class at a library or playing the guitar for children at a hospital, let's consider compensating for longer hours and longer-term commitments.

Having Witnesses in Discipline Meetings

- Traditional HR: Having a witness in progressive discipline meetings may be well-intended and can have positive outcomes. The employee might take the meeting more seriously, an additional perspective is available if the employee does something inappropriate, and the witness may help de-escalate a heated issue between the employee and their direct supervisor.
- HR Evolution: Here's when witnesses should be included:

- ○ Investigations: Yes
- ○ Terminations: Maybe
- ○ Progressive discipline: No

Witnesses are useful when concluding an investigation and sharing the outcomes with the accuser and the accused. I also think it can be helpful during a termination to have a member of the HR team present to help them understand steps with separation paperwork, collecting equipment, benefits, etc.

What is the most important work relationship? You got it–the direct supervisor. Progressive discipline allows the supervisor to own this critical part of their role, so they can help their team member understand expectations, current performance, or behavior, and partner to bridge the gap. Unless there are extenuating circumstances, such as the employee being extremely volatile and accusatory, this is best done one-on-one.

Introducing another person into this conversation can send the message that either the employee or the supervisor isn't trusted. The employee may be less receptive to feedback with another person there and may feel as though they're outnumbered or being attacked in the meeting.

Employee Handbook

- • Traditional HR: A traditional approach is as follows:
  - ○ Employees sign every time there is a change.
  - ○ More is more. We must be thorough to be compliant and clear.
  - ○ Every employee policy must be in a single handbook.

- HR Evolution:
  - Sign at hire. Save the signed handbook in their file. Include a policy that employees are responsible for understanding and following all future employee handbook updates. Store in a centralized and accessible place. Announce any changes by email and, if possible, verbally. Thus, there is no need to spend time tracking down signatures again for current employees when subsequent handbook updates are made.
  - Less is more. If the goal is understanding and compliance then we should spend considerable time making sure policies are simple, focused, and clear.
  - Store employee benefits information elsewhere. For example, insurance information changes regularly. Share that in a separate designated place and the handbook is now much shorter and needs to be updated less frequently.
  - Other departments can have their own specific policies that govern the way they work. Marketing might have brand standards, Finance will have forms and processes for managing credit cards, and Information Technology may have standards for approving different tools for people to use. Only when there is a significant overlap with the larger employee base should topics be considered for the main employee handbook.

Okay, I know I wandered right into some sensitive topics where you, your leaders, or your legal counsel may disagree with some of the evolutions here. In the spirit of simplification, maximizing our time, and being fair to others, I think they're all at least worth considering. We can escape the "that's the way we've always done it" trap and find value in considering alternatives to tradition. Just like I've been able to make great music with a five-string guitar, I've also seen great results from stepping outside the box in the workplace.

Please read this sentence out loud: "I will seek legal advice before implementing any changes in this chapter." Thank you, I feel better.

28

The Best Questions, Not the Best Answers

I don't know.

Along with "No" and "I'm sorry," "I don't know" is one of the three most empowering phrases I've learned and have (finally) given myself permission to use. I've already written a chapter on "No" ("Chapter 16: The 95 Percent Principle, Future Cory, and Other Prioritization Tools"). I've also written a chapter on "I'm sorry" ("Chapter 17: Anatomy of an Apology").

Now, let's explore why saying "I don't know" can be empowering and how to maximize its impact.

For many years in my HR career, I felt like I had to have all the answers. I spent a great deal of time learning, preparing, and trying to anticipate every question or concern I might hear in every one of my meetings or regarding any of my projects. I learned a lot; it was also exhausting. I talked more than I listened and, when I couldn't answer a question, I felt embarrassed.

Meeting Jason Fletcher changed my whole perspective. Here was an experienced and skilled leader who spent far more time asking questions and listening than he did speaking and directing. I also saw firsthand how others responded positively to the genuine interest and care in his questions. He made you feel as though you were the smartest person in the world on the topic and he was simply extracting this wisdom for everyone.

I've learned that, as HR professionals and leaders, we need the best questions, not always the best answers.

John C. Maxwell's book *Good Leaders Ask Great Questions* is a fantastic resource for learning more and finding tools. It's full of quotes that align with this idea, some from the book itself and from others that he cites:

- "The ability to ask the right question is more than half the battle of finding the answer." (Thomas J. Watson)
- "Any leader who asks the right questions of the right people has the potential to discover and develop great ideas." (John C. Maxwell)
- "Good questions inform; great questions transform." (John C. Maxwell)
- "Never miss a chance to keep your mouth shut and listen." (Robert Newton Peck)
- "One of the best ways to persuade others is with your ears." (John C. Maxwell)[1]

With that in mind, here are some of the very best questions to bring out the most in people. (I've shared a few of these in other chapters.)

Performance Management

- Is (the organization) getting your very best?
  - While I typically use this carefully with underperforming team members, this works

for employees at all performance levels, including the top performers and those who are struggling. The question is powerful because it draws a line in the sand in terms of commitment and effort. If the answer is yes from someone who's underperforming, this individual will either need more training for this role or they would be better and happier in a different role. If the answer is no, then a great follow-up is, "What can [the organization] or I do to get your very best?" This might bring out concerns about a co-worker, pay, a health concern, or some other obstacle. You can then partner with them to understand and work through the issue.

- What's next?
  - Another powerfully simple question for all performance levels. We often focus on what's wrong. Instead, asking "What's next?" opens the door for the individual to take ownership of how they would like to grow and for us to offer some ideas and observations. They might say something like public speaking or (hopefully) Microsoft Excel. We can support those and suggest, "Another area where I think you could make a big impact is making sure you're on time for all of our meetings *or* by improving the relationship you have with a specific stakeholder." Notice how it's forward and positively focused. Also, after celebrating a big win, this question keeps that momentum going.

Culture

Answer these questions about your organization and see how they correlate with your perception of its culture and whether behavior aligns with company values:

- How do senior leaders behave when they disagree?
- What kind of people thrive here?
- Are employees happy to see leaders come or happy to see them leave?

Coaching

- When's your next vacation day?
  - Our mental health is vital. Helping people set regular time off, and having something to look forward to, are important ways to maintain our mental health. By asking this question, we are advocates of their whole person. I try to ask this in all my executive coaching discussions.
- When were you the most engaged (or productive) in the last three months?
  - This can lead to a discussion about what was true at that time and how we might recreate similar conditions.
- What gets you up excited in the morning?
  - This is similar to the question above. I want to make a deliberate distinction between this and the more common question, "What keeps you up at night about work?" I prefer to focus on what's exciting because it might actually be trying to solve a big problem

at work. With this question, we can now focus on how to help them get more of that feeling.

- How would you spend one full workday if it were completely up to you?
  - I mentioned using this question in an icebreaker with a team member in Chapter 18 where we realized a team member would be much more excited about an entirely different role. I've also seen this create inclusion in an ongoing project that they had an interest in and, in another case, it helped a team member align their skills and passion with a top company priority.

Building, Rebuilding, Strengthening Relationships

- "Can I get your advice?" This is one of the most powerful questions we can ask another person to build a relationship. It's also a powerful tool to repair a relationship. This requires genuine humility to ask and a commitment to the relationship to listen with intent to act. Again, in Chapter 18, I shared my experience of starting a new job having taken someone else's job and displacing them to another office. At first, I was reluctant to ask for help because I thought I might validate their initial thoughts that I couldn't do the job or that I was too new or young to make an impact. Very soon, we forged a strong partnership, and I can trace the origins of that back to my willingness to swallow my pride and ask, "Can I get your advice?"

Self-Awareness

- Would I hire myself right now for my current role? Stitch Fix's founder and CEO, Katrina Lake, asks herself a similar question every year, and I've borrowed it. She takes time every year to evaluate what the next year will look like as the CEO and whether she will enjoy that chapter and will have the skillset to do it well. Each year when she decides to rehire herself, she starts with an open mind and the confidence that she is still the right person for the job. She will change when she reaches a point where she no longer feels like the right person.[2]

Other Topics

I'm a big believer in asking the right questions, so many of my favorite questions for other areas have been sprinkled throughout this book in different sections.

- Interview questions: "Chapter 2: Hiring for Culture 1 - Start Selection with Reflection," and "Chapter 3: Hiring for Culture 2–The Selection Spectrum"
- Delegation questions: "Chapter 13: Delegate Like a Boss"
- Reference Checks: "Chapter 27: Traditional HR vs. HR Evolutions"
- Vendor questions: "Chapter 29: Avoid Software Vendor Benders"

While being comfortable saying "I don't know" has been personally liberating, having a menu of my favorite questions to ask in different situations has been completely fulfilling. We don't have to have all the answers. Starting with the best questions will help us develop the necessary humility, relationships, and ideas to deliver on our most important outcomes.

What is your favorite question from this chapter?

_____

When will you try it out?

_____

And if you answered, "I don't know," well played.

29

Avoid Software Vendor Benders

One Sunday afternoon, I was driving our family to a local park. The park was surprisingly busy when we pulled in. As I drove down the first row of cars to find a place to park, I noticed a blue Toyota FJ Cruiser about one hundred feet in front of us, then saw a parking space up ahead that the Cruiser had just passed. The driver must have realized it, too, because they suddenly hit their brakes and began to back up. Even though I was bummed to lose that front-row spot, I patiently waited for them to back up to pull into the space. Only, they kept backing up. And backing up. They had every chance to pull in and park, yet for some reason, they kept reversing. At thirty feet, I honked. At ten feet, I honked again, longer this time until they backed right into my old Mercury Mountaineer. As I laid on the horn, I had enough time to ask my family, "What are they doing?" I was shocked.

I came out of my car to see if there was any damage to our vehicle. The other driver hopped out and said, "Oh. Sorry about that. My backup camera doesn't work." In my head, I'm thinking, *Do your eyes or ears work*?"

Thankfully, there was no damage to either vehicle and nobody was injured, so we moved on.

With modern vehicles, we often come to rely on technology (backup camera) instead of our senses (our eyes and ears), which can cause fender benders. In the workplace, we often see this with selecting software services. This same over-reliance can cause what I call "vendor benders," where a technology solution does not deliver the value expected or, worse, creates more problems.

Selecting a software vendor can be overwhelming for several reasons. These include the following:

- Falling in love with a software solution before we truly understand the problem
- Assuming that software will fix a process or people problem
- Persuasive salespeople who want to close quickly
- Many competitors and options
- Costs that vary and are complicated
- Difficulty deciding on an individual item or a whole software suite
- Choosing software that integrates with existing systems

In our roles, we are often already overwhelmed. This is likely a big reason we are seeking software support to begin with. Feeling stretched thin by the demands of responsibilities, software may seem to be a holy grail that saves time and energy. My guess is that nearly all of us can give examples of poor software solutions that are expensive, or ineffective, or cumbersome—sometimes the trifecta!

One of my companies uses a massive and expensive software solution that rhymes with "Salesforce." Originally intended as customer relationship management, which is their core purpose, they describe themselves this way, "Salesforce is a customer company. We make cloud-based software designed to help businesses connect to their customers in a whole new way, so they can find more prospects, close more deals, and wow customers with amazing service."[1] Over the years, my company modified and hard-coded Salesforce to serve multiple functions that were never intended by the software, particularly very complex and varying workflow management solutions for operations. It is now very difficult to make additional customizations and nearly impossible to transition away from it, despite the software not meeting our needs as well as we had hoped as the business grew and evolved. This is mostly on us and not necessarily on the software itself.

I've also seen sales and performance management software crash and burn after failures to launch. Often, we can trace this back to a poor selection process. So, here are some tips on how to avoid a software vendor bender:

- **No perfect system exists and never will**. Be willing to accept 80 to 90 percent of what you're hoping for by understanding the trade-offs. Jeremy Ames, our CEO, once said, "Early on in our company, we seemed to have missed an important guiding principle with software. We should have prioritized simple over perfect." Remember that: Simple over perfect.
- **Software can only help good people do good processes**. If processes are broken, these

must be fixed first. Usually, software makes bad processes worse, not better.

- Categorize wants and needs very clearly into three groups: must have, nice to have, not essential.
- **Have an owner**. Someone should clearly "own" the system so they can be the expert, help train, stay up to date on changes, manage system authorities, and so on. Make sure to listen to this person's perspectives and have them be involved in selecting the software.
- **Have multiple stakeholders involved in the decision-making**. For a Human Resources Information System (HRIS) that will impact the whole organization, consider having a member of the HR team (the owner of the system selected), at least one member of the leadership team, and a couple of people who will be users of the software, including an individual contributor.
- **"Customization" is a key buzzword for salespeople**. While this can be a good thing, it usually means a tremendous amount of work for someone on the team to design, implement, train on, and maintain the system. If a lot of customization is to be done, be ready to commit a lot of time. Customization can also make it harder to get support from the company because the support desk may not be familiar with that set-up. Ask a lot of questions about how much customization time is required and how that might impact support or access to future enhancements.
- **Buy the now**. Not the later. I can't tell you how many presentations I've sat through where a

feature I wanted was "coming in Q4" or "On our engineers' to-do list right now." Buy the now. You can't wait for what is coming because it may never come.

- **Find a way to thoroughly test the software first**. You might need to really push for access to more features and more time.
- **Operate on your timeline**. Salespeople will have goals and will likely push your decision and implementation faster than you would like. Be clear about your own timeline and operate on what will work best for you. This is especially true with implementation. The software company will likely push for a full adoption right away, whereas I've learned there is a lot more value in starting small, such as one or two departments, before a company-wide rollout.
- **Check references**. Before a final selection, ask to speak to
  - at least two clients who are currently using the software; and
  - at least one client that used their software and left their service. The company is usually surprised and reluctant with this request. I once had a salesperson tell me, "I'm not aware of anyone who has ever left." Translation: they either don't know enough about the organization, they're not being truthful, or they're new. Insist that they give you someone or search your own networks for people who had an unsatisfactory experience with the software. It's good to know why people stay; it's equally important to know why people switched.

Personally, I am very scrappy when it comes to software. Having managed multiple software systems for different organizations, I have learned that less is more. At Guidant Financial for example, we only have a payroll and timekeeping system, a simple applicant tracking system, a survey partner, and we use Microsoft Teams for company communication. All other functions are built within these tools—training, recognition, performance management, meetings, etc.

I know how much time and energy it takes for people to explore, consider, test, select, implement, train, monitor, and update a new software solution. Instead, I invest in developing people and simplifying processes.

Selecting software is a big decision. The right decision can improve everything from morale to efficiency to revenue. A poor decision can be equally costly and hard to disengage from. A complex sales process and risky decisions can be made simpler and more effective by following these tips. Now that many of us use backup cameras, let's keep using our eyes and ears, and use this feature as a reminder to not become over-reliant on technology at the expense of our senses.

Building an HR Team from Scratch

I really enjoy *The Lord of the Rings* movies. We watch them every winter, even if (or maybe because) they're so long that they sometimes take a few nights each to watch.

During the 2020 pandemic, when people were physically distancing themselves from others, we heard about many people wanting to watch movies with their families. Some wanted to watch all the Marvel movies in sequence, while others wanted to finally introduce their kids to movies they had watched when they were growing up. My family did the latter because I wanted to show my kids my favorite movie of all time. Seriously. Of. All. Time. *The Neverending Story*. Did it hold up thirty-five years later with my kids? No. Do I still love it? Absolutely. But I digress.

We had friends who decided to have movie nights with their kids to watch all *The Lord of the Rings* movies. They didn't own the movies, and none of them were available through streaming, so they asked if they could borrow our DVDs. They had never seen any of the movies and were excited. They borrowed the first one, *The Fellowship of the Ring*, and really enjoyed it, so my friend brought the disc back and took the next two movies at the same time, *The Two Towers* and *The Return of the King*. We keep the discs in a binder instead of bulky cases, so I handed them both to him in a generic clear case we kept for just such an occasion.

SPOILER ALERT! If you have not seen or read *The Lord of the Rings* and plan to, avert your eyes! Skip down to "Order matters." I even bolded it for you.

I was very curious to hear what they thought of the final two movies in the trilogy. When my friend knocked on my door to hand the movies back, I beamed, and asked, "What did you think?!"

Surprisingly, he got a puzzled look on his face. He said, "The movies were awesome, they were just a little confusing."

I responded, "I'm glad you liked them. What did you find confusing?"

He answered, "We can't figure out why they destroyed the ring in the second movie, and then in the third movie, they were back trying to destroy the ring."

Now I was confused. Then it hit me—they had watched the movies out of order! I asked, "Which movie did you watch first (of the last two)?" He opened the case and, sure enough, pointed to *The Return of the King* and said, "I think this one."

I couldn't help laughing a little bit when I explained that they had watched the movies out of order. They should have watched *The Two Towers* and then *The Return of the King*. I continued, "They're still on the path to destroy the ring in the second movie and then finally destroy it in the third." His puzzled look turned into disappointment as he realized that they had missed out on the full development of the series. I felt bad that I didn't tell him at the time which order to watch them in.

I encouraged him to watch *The Return of the King* again, which they did, somewhat redeeming their experience.

Order Matters

Because I have a passion for entrepreneurship and small business, I really enjoy helping people in this space. I have a lot of friends and people in my network who are technically small-business owners, though they may not consider themselves as such. They are dentists, chiropractors, physical therapists, and other healthcare professionals with their own practices. They go to school for many years to learn a craft, and many start their own practices without having spent much time understanding how to set up or run a business. This creates such an inspiring and fun place for me to support them and other small business owners. A question I get asked frequently from those who are growing their business is, "When should I hire Human Resources people?"

Because I am such an advocate for the HR profession, company culture, and small business, they expect me to answer somewhere between "now" and "as soon as possible." They are usually surprised and relieved by my actual answer. While there are a lot of variables such as industries, geographical locations, company culture, financial performance, etc., the following benchmarks have worked for small businesses I've consulted with. Start entry-level and have the department grow with the organization:

Growth Stage 1: Less than 15 employees

Job Title	Sample Job Functions	Additional Information
Have an amazing Human Resources professional friend or consultant.		

Growth Stage 2: 15–25 employees

Job Title	Sample Job Functions	Additional Information
Human Resources Assistant	Posting jobs, scheduling interviews, employee files, administrative support for payroll, employee benefits, onboarding, and unemployment	This could be a "hat" worn by an executive assistant or office manager-type role until this role is needed full time. I believe this role should report directly to the company's senior leader—CEO or president.
		This could be a great role to outsource. I've seen great talent for this role in the Philippines, for example. While I have a vested interest in Doxa Talent, I strongly recommend them for offshore talent. In the U.S., 15 employees is the magic number for compliance with several federal employment laws. Someone will need to have a general understanding of these laws and compliance requirements.

Growth Stage 3: 40–50 employees

Job Title	Sample Job Functions	Additional Information
Human Resources Generalist	Active recruiting role including interviews, policies and employee handbook, benefits open enrollment, employee relations, training partner, workers compensation, coordinating culture activities, leave management	The HR generalist should report directly to the company's senior leader. The senior leader, the HR generalist, and the HR assistant will make up the Human Resources team. The HR generalist role can start as or evolve into a lead role for the HR assistant, which will likely need to shift to a full-time commitment at this stage.
		The word *generalist* isn't familiar to most small-business owners and sounds strange to some in a job title. It's a legit and healthy part of the HR career ecosystem. Hire an absolute rock star here, with a few years' experience. Pay and treat them well. Develop them into the next role. Will need legal support.

Growth Stage 4: 75–100 employees

Job Title	Sample Job Functions	Additional Information
Human Resources Manager	All aspects of Human Resources Supports culture and executes HR strategy Key HR metrics Excellent recruiting support, especially for senior-level and niche roles Focus on effectiveness, compliance, infrastructure, and processes for HR department	Promote your rock star Human Resources generalist! Or hire a great person externally. Still report to company's senior leader. Has the HR Generalist and HR Assistant roles reporting to them. May need legal support.

Growth Stage 5: Over 100 employees

Job Title	Sample Job Functions	Additional Information
Human Resources Director	Drives and leads all HR strategy, organizational design, metrics, talent management, the culture steward, participates as a senior leader in discussions/decisions, executive coach	Promote your rock star Human Resources manager! Still reports to senior leader. Leads HR team. May need to decide how to grow, with specialists or generalists based on the needs of the business. May need less legal support.

According to Indeed, "An average HR staff to employee ratio is around 2.57 for all organizations. Small organizations have higher ratios with an average of 3.40. Medium organizations often have ratios around 1.22 while a normal ratio for large organizations is 1.03."[1] Here is the formula:

Number of HR Professionals / Total employees x 100

Let's look at growth stage 4, hypothetically with three full-time HR team members and ninety-five employees:

3 / 95 x 100 = 3.16

This 3.16 is less than the 3.4 average for small organizations suggested by Indeed.

My framework for this hypothetical small business maximizes the ability to invest in hiring excellent people right away for these early roles.

I'll address head-on the recommendation to have HR report directly to the senior leader throughout the growth of the HR department. Like marketing and sales, where two departments are distinct yet must be symbiotic for both to succeed, HR must have a similar healthy tension between other departments to maximize all functions. I've had the privilege of working with some amazing finance and operations professionals in my career, yet I believe we should avoid the temptation to funnel the HR function through any other departments. That way, we can retain the healthy tension and symbiosis that brings the right balance to important conversations and decisions.

After I had been an HR director for a few years, an acquaintance who had just started a business wanted to take me to lunch to get my advice on a few key areas because he had just hired his first employee. I wasn't expecting him to ask me to come on board as his HR director and second employee. I absolutely loved his passion for his business, his belief in the power of the

HR function, and his trust in me. One reason behind my recommended plan is that an HR director hired at his stage of the business would end up doing short-term administrative work instead of the long-term strategic work that justifies the salary level. Because he was willing to hire me at my salary, I encouraged him to invest in an amazing HR assistant instead and give them lots of room to grow, contribute, and earn more. That would be the best outcome for both parties at that stage.

Order matters.

31

An End and a Beginning

One summer, I went camping and fishing in the beautiful Idaho mountains with some of my best friends. It was me and my friend Mike's first time fly fishing, and we both caught our first fish, just in a different way than you are thinking. Mike had the fly rod while I was armed with a different weapon: a snorkel mask. Because we were woefully inexperienced, I swam in the very cold river with my mask and pointed Mike to different areas in the river where I could see fish. It sounds ridiculous, and it was! While I apologize to any fly-fishing purists, I also want to acknowledge that it was very fun to catch and release in the middle fork of the Boise River that day. We have a very funny picture of both of us holding up the small fish we caught "together."

Sometimes we feel inadequate, new, confused, or overwhelmed, and we need someone to point us in the right direction, like I did with Mike that day fishing.

Sometimes we think we're doing a good job, following best practices, and getting good results, and we need someone to validate our efforts and outcomes.

Sometimes we need to hear new stories and perspectives to laugh and enjoy the journey of leadership, Human Resources, and life.

Sometimes we need to have a trusted partner to take a similar journey with.

If you have read this whole book, I feel like we now have a special shared experience and I hope I checked all the "sometimes" boxes above. In the Preface, I mentioned that I hope you experience the following:

1. Feel empowered and confident to try something new from over one hundred different practical tips and become inspired to be part of a large group that is trying to get better every day in leadership and Human Resources roles.
2. Feel validated and celebrated for the great work you are already doing, especially when you read something in the book that's working well for you.
3. Have fun. I hope you enjoy the book enough to have some new stories and examples to think about, laugh about, and apply in different ways. Laughter accelerates learning.
4. Have a desire to reach out to me—I want to know what works for you, what you've tried that didn't go as you expected, and I am always a fan of funny stories. Send them to HRYouKiddingMe@ gmail.com or let's connect on LinkedIn: https:// www.linkedin.com/in/Cory-Sanford.

For fifteen years at U.S. Bank, then Ada County, then Ashley Manor/Auburn Crest Hospice, I voluntarily wore a tie to work every day. Every. Day. I even have pictures of me doing a challenging ropes course as a team-building exercise with my tie, slacks, and dress shoes on.

I always wanted to look and feel professional. I felt the tie elevated my professionalism, my behavior, and my results. Naturally, I wore a tie for all my interviews with Guidant Financial, where I noticed I was the only person with a tie. The culture was different. Not better or worse, just different. When I was offered the job, I had a choice about how to dress. I decided to skip the tie. It was a new beginning for me and taking off the tie symbolized my motivation to keep trying new things, keep getting better, and to keep evolving my thinking. It also helped me feel part of the culture instead of trying to stand out by wearing a tie.

It's taken me a long time to learn what I've shared in this book, and I work hard every day to live up to my own expectations and advice. I'm not perfect, and I appreciate everyone who's given me grace when I have fallen short.

The end of a book always marks the beginning of a new way of thinking and applying new ideas. Here's a chance for you to reflect:

What was your favorite new tip, tool, framework, or idea you are excited to try? When and where will you try it first?

_____

_____

_____

What is your favorite part of the book that validates something you're already doing well?

_____

_____

_____

What is your favorite story from the book? What made this story stand out for you?

_____

_____

_____

Who can you share your commitments with to help you keep growing? By what date will you do this?

_____

_____

_____

Now let's end where we started—with me as a six-year-old with two broken wrists. Strangely, my daughter Skylee broke one of her arms in first grade falling from the monkey bars—something I wasn't expecting to pass down to one of my children. Here is a picture of my casts:

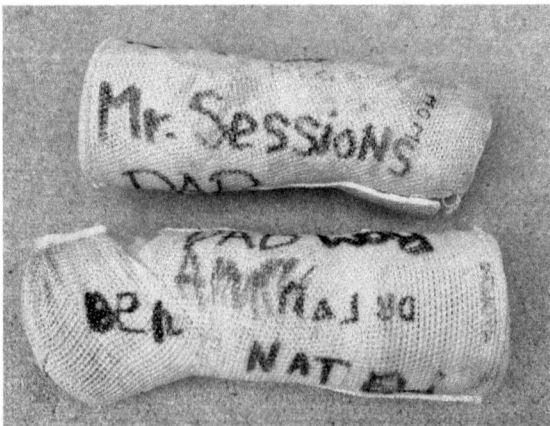

Notice that Mr. Sessions signed it biggest. He finally believed me! Also, see Ben's name. Let's be the Ben in someone else's life: supportive, compassionate, patient, and brave.

My personal motto is, "I am infinitely optimistic about the potential of people." I have seen ordinary people do extraordinary things. They didn't do them alone, and people will continue to do extraordinary things if they have others who believe in them and are committed to supporting them.

I believe the workplace should be where people can be their best, do their best, and feel their best. Let us be the reason that somebody believes more and achieves more. It is as rewarding a path as I have found.

Keep having fun and making an impact, my friends!

Acknowledgments

In addition to the wonderful leaders I've had the privilege of working with, to whom this book is dedicated, I have had the honor of working with some of the greatest teammates on this planet. Thank you to everyone at Ada County, Ashley Manor, Auburn Crest Home Health and Hospice, Guidant Financial, and Cornell University. Our interactions have shaped me for the better.

Specifically, I want to thank the following:

- Ada County: Bethany Calley, Kim Osborn, Cassie Danell, Rich Wright, Suzanne Guinard, and Phil McGrane
- Ashley Manor: Keith Fletcher, Stacy Gunnerson, Stacy Tennant, Jenna Gordon, Kathi Brink, Dave Martin, Shannon Jansen, and Kathleen Baity
- Auburn Crest Home Health and Hospice: Jason Fletcher, Mike Haycraft, and Jared Hess
- Guidant Financial: Jeremy Ames, David Nilssen, Lauren Hoover, Katie Burckhardt, Jared Weed, Michelle Flandreau, Devin Miller, Laura Paradis, Jason Baker, Jessica Kirkendall, Skye Asbach, Jen Dai, T.A. McCann, and Nick Collins
- Cornell University: Chris Collins, Brad Bell, Cathy Pantano, Will Conaway, and the entire Executive Master of Human Resource Management cohort of 2019
- Other mentors: Michael Glauser, Gundars Kaupins, Dusty Bodie, Tonn Petersen, Alinka Rutkowska, and Michelle Beauchamp

I am grateful for my author friends who took the time to share their experience and wisdom with me: Johnna Johnson (author of *Just Jump!*), Brian Fretwell (*Experts of Our Potential*), Lex Sisney (*Organizational Physics and Designed to Scale*), Jeremy Graves (*The Leader Paradox*), and Rick Orford (*The Financially Independent Millennial*).

This book literally wouldn't exist if it weren't for Joshua Dewaine Foster, my writing accountability partner, and author of *The Crown Package*. We checked in every week for many months on goals and progress with our projects. He gave me sound guidance, encouragement, continuous support, and helped me live the 5 Pillars of Behavior Change (5 Ps).

Finally, and most importantly, I must thank my family for their support my whole life with my quirkiness, embarrassing them (usually on purpose, sometimes on accident), and allowing me to grow into who I am today. They have graciously allowed me to reference them in these pages and were incredibly supportive during the time I took to write and publish this book. Taryn, the love of my life, is an angel who somehow did even more for our family while I spent time writing. She even made time to be the first editor of this book and has motivated me the whole way.

I love you all!

Appendix

From Chapter 6: Culture Is Connection – Activity description
Connection to Purpose
Required

1. **Monday Morning Stand-up**. Every Monday morning, we have an all-company Zoom meeting hosted by a senior leader. This is a great chance to report on performance and key initiatives, recognize accomplishments, welcome new team members, thank departing team members, and share any other important information regarding the business internally or outside factors that could impact the company or our clients.

2. **Remote Code of Conduct**. A comprehensive guide that covers areas such as responsiveness, which includes promptly answering emails and being available during designated work hours. We also have expectations regarding video availability, such as being willing to participate in video conferences and having cameras turned on during meetings. We have set expectations regarding internet requirements. We also encourage employees to take care of themselves and promote a healthy work-life balance.

3. **Quarterly Engagement Survey**: We use Survey Monkey to send quarterly surveys to our team. See "Chapter 21: People Hate Surveys for my thoughts on surveys."

Optional

1. **Client Testimonials**. We love showcasing the positive impact we've made on clients and the positive impact those clients have made in their own lives and in their communities. These are available on our website and in our Employee Resource Center whenever our team members are interested in getting inspired.
2. **Swag**. At least once per year we send all team members some new company-branded gear like shirts, hoodies, hats, bandannas, stickers, water bottles, etc. Wearing this reminds us of our collective purpose.
3. **Employee Resource Center**. I've used both Microsoft Teams and Dropbox to create a convenient, centralized location for team members to access current information about the company and their roles. This includes company values, strategic plans, guiding principles, and client testimonials. People can also find employee handbooks, job descriptions, and employee benefits information.

Connection to Leaders
Required

1. **People Celebrations**. Twice each year, we spend an hour celebrating our team members by providing awards based on specific examples of living core values in the preceding six months. Senior leaders recognize each winner and share those examples that led to their nomination and selection.

2. **Regular Supervisor One-on-Ones**. See "Chapter 11: The Silver Bullet in Leadership*" for more information.

Optional

1. **Leadership Coffee**. Every quarter, team members have the opportunity to sign up to have "coffee" with a senior leader and a small group of peers. These are casual interactions where the leader has the flexibility to discuss anything they choose. Some are work-related, some are more personal, some are fun, some are serious, and sometimes games are played.
2. **Weekly CEO Email**. Every week, the CEO sends an email to the entire company sharing good news, recognizing team members for living company values and principles and/or achieving great results, and providing key business updates.

Connection to Each Other
Required

1. **Monthly Team Building Budget**. Each supervisor is provided a monthly amount to spend on connecting. This can be lunches, recognition, birthday gifts, a virtual activity, etc.
2. **Regular Team Meetings**. These occur at least monthly.
3. **Annual All-Day Event**. Every year we close the office to have a full day connecting and learning together.
4. **Pictures in Microsoft Teams.** In Dan Pink's book *To Sell Is Human*, he shares a fascinating study by

Israeli radiologist Yehonatan Turner. The study concludes that radiologists were 80 percent more accurate when a picture of the person accompanied the X-ray.[1] We use Microsoft Teams as a primary means of communication, so each person is required to have an avatar picture to bring a more human connection into each interaction.

Optional

1. **Monthly People Newsletter**. This contains information about birthdays, anniversaries, our monthly focus principle, upcoming events, team spotlights, promotions, and other good news.
2. **Microsoft Teams Channels**
   - Cheers! – This channel is designated for peer-to-peer recognition, and we encourage each recognition to tie to a value or guiding principle. This channel is very active.
   - Breakroom – This channel is intended to re-create a breakroom in an office where you might bump into somebody and chat about recipes, vacations, kids, pets, or the weather.
3. **Employee Committees**
   - Connection, Opportunity, and Growth (COG) – This committee supports a variety of different events and activities to keep us connected. They host monthly connection events and are active in our Breakroom Teams channel.
   - Diversity, Equity, and Inclusion (DEI) – This committee creates opportunities for us to learn about and celebrate people's unique backgrounds, experiences, heritage, and

history. Among many other activities, they share a weekly post and create quarterly discussion opportunities.

Chapter 8: The Playbook for a Fully Remote Transition
Criteria for evaluating U.S. states for relocation

1. **Policy**. Someone must be with Guidant for at least three years and be in good standing.
2. **Criteria**. We evaluate financial criteria such as taxes, fees, and other costs of operating a business in that state, which usually depends on how that state views different types of entities. We also evaluate employment laws such as at-will, payroll timing requirements, sick leave, break requirements, overtime calculations, work-from-home regulations, final paycheck timing, and others. We believe we have fair and consistent practices and want to make sure that each new state fits within our current policies so that they are easier to administer.
3. **Administrative Costs**. Even in the best-case scenario, where a state meets all the financial and employment law criteria, there are several administrative costs to consider:
   - HR and Finance teams creating and maintaining accounts, reports, payments, etc. for unemployment insurance, workers' compensation, and state payroll taxes.
   - Additional state, and sometimes city, corporate and/or sales taxes, with the additional risk of time-consuming and costly audits. Often these costs and filings are indefinite, whether employees remain in that state or not.

- Depending upon the business entity, each company shareholder may need to file a personal income tax in that state each year.
- The risk of the state, or any city or county within that state, to develop additional finance, legal, or HR laws that would require communication, implementation, and continued compliance.

4. **Another Option**. We have a payrolling partner that team members can transfer to as their official employer if they want to continue working for our company and move to a state outside of our approved footprint. The team members retain their pay, PTO balance, and accrual rate. One trade-off is the retirement and insurance offerings are different.

Notes and References

Preface

1. Gitomer, Jeffrey. *The Little Book of Leadership*. John Wiley & Sons, Inc, 2011.

Chapter 1
The Role of Human Resources

1. "Toby Flenderson." Dunderpedia: The Office Wiki. Accessed July 20, 2023. https://theoffice.fandom. com/wiki/Toby_Flenderson
2. "Workforce Management: The 5 Main Roles in HR." Paycor, Inc. Last modified June 27, 2022. https://www. paycor.com/resource-center/articles/the-5-main-roles-in-hr/#:~:text=Human%20Resources%20 manages%205%20main,effectively%20managing %20the%20employee%20lifecycle
3. Cooke, Nick. "What Does Human Resources Do? (With 12 Key Functions)." Indeed. Last modified July 20, 2023. https://www.indeed.com/career-advice/ finding-a-job/what-does-human-resources-do
4. OpenAI. "The Role of Human Resources." ChatGPT. Asked July 21, 2023. https://openai.com/chatgpt
5. Marquet, L. David, and Stephen R. Covey. *Turn the Ship Around!: A True Story of Turning Followers into Leaders*. 1st ed. USA: Portfolio, 2013.

Chapter 2
Hiring for Culture 1—Start Selection with Reflection

1. Freija. "Construction Workers Needed." iFunny. June 30, 2023. https://ifunny.co/picture/construction-workers-needed-lake-fork-area-plea-do-not-apply-jmKxAsfcA

Chapter 3
Hiring for Culture 2—The Selection Spectrum

1. Gandhi, Vipula, and Jennifer Robison. "The 'Great Resignation' Is Really the 'Great Discontent'." Workplace. July 22, 2021.https://www.gallup.com/workplace/351545/great-resignation-really-great-discontent.aspx
2. Frye, Lisa. "The Cost of a Bad Hire Can Be Astronomical." SHRM. May 9, 2017. https://www.shrm.org/resourcesandtools/hr-topics/employee-relations/pages/cost-of-bad-hires.aspx
3. Neugaard, Britta. "Halo Effect: Psychology." Britannica. Last Modified August 25, 2023. https://www.britannica.com/science/halo-effect

Chapter 4:
Good Onboarding Is the Best Recruiting Insurance

1. Miller, Stephen. "SHRM HR Benchmarking Reports Launch as a Free Member-Exclusive Benefit." SHRM. April 11, 2022. https://www.shrm.org/resourcesandtools/hr-topics/benefits/pages/shrm-hr-benchmarking-reports-launch-as-a-member-exclusive-benefit.aspx

2. Penn, Rick, and Victor Huang. "Job Openings Reach Record Highs in 2022 as the Labor Market Recovery Continues." U.S. Bureau of Labor Statistics. May 2023. https://www.bls.gov/opub/mlr/2023/article/job-openings-reach-record-highs-in-2022-as-the-labor-market-recovery-continues.htm#:~:text=Hires%20 have%20continued%20to%20increase,was%20 4.2%20percent%20in%202022

3. "Lloyds of London – The Home of Quirky and Unusual Insurance." McClarrons Sport Ltd. Accessed May 8, 2023. https://www.mcclarroninsurance.com/news/ quirky-insurance-risks/

4. Jaramillo, Janine. "The Science and Power of First Impressions." The University of Melbourne. October 22, 2021. https://blogs.unimelb.edu.au/science-communication/2021/10/22/the-science-and-power-of-first-impressions/

Chapter 5
Offboarding Is the New Onboarding

1. "St Luke's advertisement for Job Openings." *Idaho Statesman newspaper*, Accessed September 13, 2023. Fieldstadt, Elisha. "Feds sue auto repair shop that paid former employee in pennies." *NBC Universal*, January 7, 2022. https://www.nbcnews. com/news/feds-sue-auto-repair-shop-paid-former-employee-pennies-rcna11339

2. "An HR Glossary for HR Terms: Glossary of Human Resources Management and Employee Benefit Terms." Bamboo HR LLC. Accessed June 19, 2023. https://www.bamboohr.com/resources/hr-glossary/ boomerang-employee

3. Miles, Madeline. "In a Tight Labor Market, Don't Overlook Boomerang Employees." BetterUp. April 7,

2022. https://www.betterup.com/blog/boomerang-employee

Chapter 6
Culture Is Connection

1. "2023 Best Places to Work in Idaho – Statewide." Best Places to Work in Idaho. Accessed May 3, 2023. https://www.bestplacestoworkinidaho.com/winners/statewide/

Chapter 7
Infusing Core Values Through the Whole Organization

1. Kadlec, Daniel. "Enron: Who's Accountable?." *TIME USA*, January 13, 2002. https://content.time.com/time/subscriber/article/0,33009,1001636,00.html

2. Markel, Howard. "How the Tylenol Murders of 1982 Changed the Way We Consume Medication." *PBSO NewsHour*, September 29, 2014. https://www.pbs.org/newshour/health/tylenol-murders-1982

3. McCreary, Matthew. "Chick-fil-A Makes More Per Restaurant than McDonald's, Starbucks and Subway Combined … and It's Closed on Sundays." Entrepreneur Media. Modified February 26, 2020. https://www.entrepreneur.com/franchises/chick-fil-a-makes-more-per-restaurant-than-mcdonalds/320615

4. "Why is Chick-fil-A closed on Sunday?." Chick-fil-A One. Accessed August 28, 2023. https://www.chick-fil-a.com/sunday-videom

5. Groysberg, Boris, Jeremiah Lee, Jesse Price, and J. Yo-Jud Cheng. "The Leader's Guide to Corporate Culture." *Harvard Business Review*, February 2018. https://hbr.org/2018/01/the-culture-factor

6. Dalio, Ray. "Principles: Your Guided Journal." Principles. Accessed September 10, 2023. https://www.principles.com/

Chapter 8
The Playbook for a Fully Remote Transition

1. Mollman, Steve. "OpenAI CEO Sam Altman says the Remote work 'Experiment' was a Mistake—and 'it's Over'." Fortune. May 5, 2023. https://fortune.com/2023/05/05/openai-ceo-sam-altman-remote-work-mistake-return-to-office/
2. Forbes Contributors. "Disney CEO Bob Iger Requires Hybrid Staff to Return to the Office at Least Four Days a Week - Here's How Employees and Investors have Responded." Forbes. Accessed May 9, 2023. https://www.forbes.com/sites/qai/2023/01/18/disney-ceo-bob-iger-requires-hybrid-staff-to-return-to-the-office-at-least-four-days-a-weekheres-how-employees-and-investors-have-responded/?sh=f815fd723226
3. Biron, Bethany. "Starbucks CEO Howard Schultz says, 'I'll get on my knees' and 'do whatever you want,' Pleading with Workers to Return to the Office." Insider. June 11, 2022. https://www.businessinsider.com/starbucks-ceo-howard-schultz-begs-workers-return-office-2022-6

Chapter 9
Seattle Mariners or Colorado Rockies

1. "Information Guide." Colorado Rockies. Accessed September 20, 2023. https://www.mlb.com/rockies/ballpark/information/guide - retrieved 4/30/2023

Chapter 10
Death by Acronyms

1. Ziglar, Tom. The Gratitude Moment. Ziglar. Accessed April 29, 2023. https://www.ziglar.com/articles/the-gratitude-moment/

Chapter 11
The Silver Bullet in Leadership*

1. Goleman, Daniel, Richard E. Boyatzis, and Annie McKee. *Primal Leadership: Unleashing the Power of Emotional Intelligence.* Boston: Harvard Business Review Press, 2013.
2. Royle, Orianna Rosa. "Managers Impact Employees' Mental Health More than Therapists and as Much as a Spouse or Partner. Here's how Bosses can Spark Change in Conversations." Fortune. February 6, 2023. https://fortune.com/2023/02/06/managers-impact-worker-mental-health-more-than-therapists-research-shows-bosses-change-conversation/

Chapter 12
E.A.S.E. into More Effectiveness

1. Townsend, Robert. *Up the Organization: How to Stop the Corporation from Stifling People and Strangling Profits.* New York: Alfred A. Knopf, 1970.
2. Sullivan, Dan, and Benjamin Hardy. *Who Not How: The Formula to Achieve Bigger Goals Through Accelerating Teamwork.* Hay House Business, 2020

Chapter 13
Delegate Like a Boss

1. Zander, Benjamin. "TED: The transformative power of classical music – Transcript." TED. Accessed June 1, 2023. https://www.benjaminzander.org/uploads/2020/07/TED_-The-transformative-power-of-classical-music-Transcript.pdf

2. United States Department of Labor. "Economic New Release: Job Openings and Labor Turnover Summary." U.S. Bureau of Labor Statistics. Last Modified October 03, 2023. https://www.bls.gov/news.release/jolts.nr0.htm

3. Smith, Morgan. "Gen Z and Millennials are Leading 'the Big Quit' in 2023–Why Nearly 70% Plan to Leave their Jobs." CNBC LLC. January 18, 2023. https://www.cnbc.com/2023/01/18/70percent-of-gen-z-and-millennials-are-considering-leaving-their-jobs-soon.html

4. Kumar, Vibha S. "Gen Z In The Workplace: How Should Companies Adapt?." Johns Hopkins University. April 18, 2023. https://imagine.jhu.edu/blog/2023/04/18/gen-z-in-the-workplace-how-should-companies-adapt/

5. Liu, Jennifer. "1 in 4 Workers is Considering Quitting their Job after the Pandemic–here's why. CNBC LLC. April 19, 2021. https://www.cnbc.com/2021/04/19/1-in-4-workers-is-considering-quitting-their-job-after-the-pandemic.html

6. Chenault, Ken. "Business Lessons from American Express CEO Ken Chenault." NP Digital, LLC. Accessed June 1, 2023. https://neilpatel.com/blog/lessons-from-ken-chenault/

7. Maxwell, John. *The 5 Levels of Leadership: Proven Steps to Maximize Your Potential.* New York, NY: Center Street, 2013.

8. Maxwell, John. *The 5 Levels of Leadership: Proven Steps to Maximize Your Potential.* New York, NY: Center Street, 2013.

9. Covey, Stephan R. *The 7 Habits of Highly Effective People: Powerful Lessons in Personal Change.* Free Press, 2004.

10. Marquet, L. David, and Stephen R. Covey. *Turn the Ship Around!: A True Story of Turning Followers into Leaders.* 1st ed. USA: Portfolio, 2013.

Chapter 14
P.O.S.E. the Problem

1. "Roatán, Honduras – Sunrise, Sunset, and Day length." Time and Date AS. October 3, 2023. https://www.timeanddate.com/sun/honduras/roatan

2. Mind Tool content Team. "5 Ways Route-Cause Analysis." Mind Tools. Accessed August 15, 2023. https://www.mindtools.com/a3mi00v/5-whys

3. Koppel, Ted, Jack Smith, ABC News, and Films for the Humanities Firm. "The Deep Dive: One Company's Secret Weapon for Innovation." Films for the Humanities & Sciences. 2004. https://films.com/ecTitleDetail.aspx?TitleID=11160

4. Boyle, Brendan. "7 Simple Rules of Brainstorming." IDEO. Accessed September 20, 2023. https://www.ideou.com/blogs/inspiration/7-simple-rules-of-brainstorming

5. About Us: IDEO is a Global Design Company. IDEO. Accessed June 11, 2023. https://www.ideo.com/about

6. Boyle, Brendan. "7 Simple Rules of Brainstorming." IDEO. Accessed September 20, 2023. https://www. ideou.com/blogs/inspiration/7-simple-rules-of-brainstorming

7. Maslow, Abraham H., and Arthur G. Wirth. *The Psychology of Science: A Reconnaissance*. New York: Harper & Row, 1966.

Chapter 15
Positivizing Our Communication

1. Sudeikis, Jason, Brendan Hunt, Joe Kelly, Jeff Ingold, and Bill Wrubel, producer. *Ted Lasso*. Season 1, Episode 2, "Biscuits with the Boss." Directed by Declan Lowney, featuring Jason Sudeikis, Hannah Waddingham, Jeremy Swift, Phil Dunster, Brett Goldstein, Brendan Hunt, Nick Mohammed, Juno Temple, Sarah Niles, Anthony Head, Toheeb Jimoh, Cristo Fernández, Kola Bokinni, Billy Harris, and James Lance. Aired August 14, 2020, in Apple TV, https://tv.apple.com/us/show/ted-lasso/umc.cmc. vtoh0mn0xn7t3c643xqonfzy.

2. Mind Tool content Team. "5 Ways Route-Cause Analysis." Mind Tools. Accessed August 15, 2023. https://www.mindtools.com/a3mi00v/5-whys

Chapter 16
The 95 Percent Principle, Future Cory, and Other Prioritization Tools

1. Yo Gabba Gabba! - WildBrain. "Yo Gabba Gabba 101 - Eat". YouTube. https://www.youtube.com/watch?v=2YN8bUHufPk

2. McChesney, Chris, Sean Covey, and Jim Huling. *The 4 Disciplines of Execution: Achieving Your Wildly Important Goals*. New York: Free Press, 2012.
3. McChesney, Chris, Sean Covey, and Jim Huling. *The 4 Disciplines of Execution: Achieving Your Wildly Important Goals*. New York: Free Press, 2012.
4. Covey, Stephen R. *Principle-Centered Leadership*. Simon and Schuster, 1992.
5. Bays, Carter, Craig Thomas, and Gloria Calderón Kellett, writer. *The Duel*. Season 1 Episode 8, "How I Met Your Mother." Directed by Pamela Fryman, featuring Josh Radnor, Jason Segel, and Cobie Smulders. Aired November 14, 2005, in IMDb, https://www.imdb.com/title/tt0606113/
6. "I am Learning to Love the Sound of My Feet Walking Away from Things not Meant for Me." Daily Inspirational Quotes. Accessed June 19, 2023. https://www.dailyinspirationalquotes.in/2018/07/i-am-learning-to-love-the-sound-of-my-feet-walking-away-from-things-not-meant-for-me/

Chapter 18
Your Secret Weapon

1. Carnegie, Dale. *How to Win Friends and Influence People*. New York: Simon & Schuster, 2009.
2. Andrews, Andy. *The Seven Decisions: Understanding the Keys to Personal Success*. Thomas Nelson, 2014.
3. Maxwell, John. *The 5 Levels of Leadership: Proven Steps to Maximize Your Potential*. New York, NY: Center Street, 2013.
4. Marmolejo-Ramos, Fernando, Aiko Murata, Kyoshiro Sasaki, Yuki Yamada, Ayumi Ikeda, José A. Hinojosa, Katsumi Watanabe, Michal Parzuchowski, Carlos Tirado, and Raydonal Ospina. "Your Face and

Moves Seem Happier When I Smile: Facial Action Influences the Perception of Emotional Faces and Biological Motion Stimuli." 67, no. 1 (2020): 14-22. https://kyushu-u.elsevierpure.com/en/publications/your-face-and-moves-seem-happier-when-i-smile-facial-action-influ

5. Goleman, Daniel, Richard E. Boyatzis, and Annie McKee. *Primal Leadership: Unleashing the Power of Emotional Intelligence.* Boston: Harvard Business Review Press, 2013.

6. Favreau, Jon, dir. *Elf.* 2003; United Kingdom, UK: New Line Cinema, 2003. https://www.imdb.com/title/tt0319343/

Chapter 19
What a Bank Robber Taught Me about Training

1. Glauser, Michael J., interview, 2003 (specific date unknown)

2. Covey, Stephan R. *The 7 Habits of Highly Effective People: Powerful Lessons in Personal Change.* Free Press, 2004.

3. Maravich, Pete. "I Want to Put on a Show." Vault. December 1, 1969. https://vault.si.com/vault/1969/12/01/i-want-to-put-on-a-show

4. Phillips, Patricia P. *ASTD Handbook of Measuring and Evaluating Training.* Alexandria, VA: American Society for Training and Development, 2010.

Chapter 20
My Dream Job Description

1. Mohr, Tara S. "Why Women Don't Apply for Jobs unless they're 100% Qualified." *Harvard Business*

Review, August 25, 2014. https://hbr.org/2014/08/
why-women-dont-apply-for-jobs-unless-theyre-
100-qualified

2. White, Martha C. "The U.S. Now has More Job
Openings than Any Time in History." *NBC News*,
August 9, 2021. https://www.nbcnews.com/
business/business-news/u-s-now-has-more-job-
openings-any-time-history-n1276367

Chapter 22
The Reasons Bonuses Aren't Working

1. Doherty, Patricia. "The Ultimate Country-by-Country
Guide to Tipping in Europe." Travel+ Leisure. July
2, 2022. https://www.travelandleisure.com/travel-
tips/guide-to-tipping-in-europe-hotels-restaurants-
taxis-tours

2. Sinek, Simon. *Start With Why*. UK: Penguin Random
House, 2009

3. Pink, Daniel H. *Drive: The Surprising Truth about What
Motivates Us*. New York, NY: Penguin Publishing
Group, 2011.

4. Segal, Peter, dir. *Tommy Boy movie*. 1995; United
Kingdom, UK: Broadway Pictures, 1995. https://
www.imdb.com/title/tt0114694/

5. Bowles, Samuel. "When Economic Incentives Backfire." *Harvard Business Review,* March 2009. https://
hbr.org/2009/03/when-economic-incentives-back-
fire

6. Lytle, Tamara. "When Employee Incentives Go
Wrong." SHRM. April 22, 2023. https://www.shrm.
org/hr-today/news/all-things-work/pages/when-
employee-incentives-go-wrong.aspx

7. Hale, Justin. "Incentives Gone Wrong: How
Leaders Mishandle Pay and Perks." Forbes.

November 21, 2022. https://www.forbes.com/sites/forbescoachescouncil/2022/11/21/incentives-gone-wrong-how-leaders-mishandle-pay-and-perks/?sh=9223c6162084

8. Rolnick, Matthew. "Beware of the "Cobra Effect" in Business." Forbes. August 26, 2020. https://www.forbes.com/sites/forbesbusinessdevelopment-council/2020/08/26/beware-of-the-cobra-effect-in-business/?sh=122ba7e35f6f

9. Office of Public Affairs. "Wells Fargo Agrees to Pay $3 Billion to Resolve Criminal and Civil Investigations into Sales Practices Involving the Opening of Millions of Accounts without Customer Authorization." U.S. Department of Justice. February 21, 2020. https://www.justice.gov/opa/pr/wells-fargo-agrees-pay-3-billion-resolve-criminal-and-civil-investigations-sales-practices

10. Collins, Jim. *Good to Great: Why Some Companies Make the Leap and Others Don't*. United States: HarperBusiness, 2001.

11. RSA. "RSA Animate: Drive: The surprising Truth about What Motivates Us." YouTube. https://www.youtube.com/watch?v=u6XAPnuFjJc&t=397s

Chapter 23
The Language of HR: Data

1. "Gallup's Employee Engagement Survey: Ask the Right Questions with the Q12® Survey." GALLUP. Accessed July 14, 2023.https://www.gallup.com/workplace/356063/gallup-q12-employee-engagement-survey.aspx?utm_source=google&utm_medium=cpc&utm_campaign=gallup_access_brand-ed&utm_term=gallup%20q12%20 questions&gclid= CjwKCAjw5MOlBhBTEiwAAJ8e1nXa cnOgj2PkxRPR

7b5B_IO7S0C2-i41i2ZdgtA-ciaYWrc1pRd1Xxo-CIAQQAvD_BwE

2. "The difference Between Quantitative vs. Qualitative Research." Survey Monkey. Accessed July 13, 2023. https://www.surveymonkey.com/mp/quantitative-vs-qualitative-research/

3. McChesney, Chris, Sean Covey, and Jim Huling. *The 4 Disciplines of Execution: Achieving Your Wildly Important Goals*. New York: Free Press, 2012.

4. Quoteresearch. If I Had More Time, I Would Have Written a Shorter Letter." Quote Investigator. April 28, 2012. https://quoteinvestigator.com/2012/04/28/shorter-letter/

5. Nationwide Pet, "Nationwide Pet's Post: Voluntary Benefits, Offer Employee Pet Insurance Plans, Nationwide," LinkedIn, 2020, https://www.linkedin.com/feed/update/urn:li:activity:6669288566658621440/

Chapter 24
Employee "Real"ations

1. Sudeikis, Jason, Brendan Hunt, Joe Kelly, Jeff Ingold, and Bill Wrubel, producer. *Ted Lasso*. Season 1, Episode 5, "Rainbow". Directed by Declan Lowney, featuring Jason Sudeikis, Hannah Waddingham, Jeremy Swift, Phil Dunster, Brett Goldstein, Brendan Hunt, Nick Mohammed, Juno Temple, Sarah Niles, Anthony Head, Toheeb Jimoh, Cristo Fernández, Kola Bokinni, Billy Harris, and James Lance. Aired August 19, 2021, in Apple TV, https://tv.apple.com/us/episode/rainbow/umc.cmc.2wrxmrfpkz6yqc38lokscruw4

2. Bentley, Paul. "Professional and Continuing Education." Boise State University. 2015. https://www.boisestate.edu/pace/

3. Grenny, Joseph, Kerry Patterson, Ron McMillan, Al Switzler, and Emily Gregory. *Crucial Conversations: Tools for Talking When Stakes are High*. New York, NY: McGraw Hill, 2001.

Chapter 25
"Unlimited" Paid Time Off Exposed

1. "Netflix Jobs: Work Life Balance." Netflix. Accessed June 22, 2023. https://jobs.netflix.com/work-life-philosophy

2. Wood, Anthony. "Roku Culture." Roku. May 2015. https://image.roku.com/ww/press/2015/Roku_Culture_2015.pdf

3. Nguyen, Lananh, and Emma Goldberg. "Goldman's Move to Unlimited Vacation Is Good for … Goldman." *New York Times*, May 27, 2022. https://www.nytimes.com/2022/05/27/business/goldman-sachs-unlimited-vacation.html

4. Interview with anonymous source. August 6th, 2019.

5. Interview with anonymous source. August 10th, 2019.

6. Johnson, Richard. "1 in 2 Professionals Can't Fully Unplug on Their Vacation." Glassdoor. July 12, 2022. https://www.glassdoor.com/research/professionals-cant-fully-unplug-on-vacation/

7. Luca, Rob de. "How Does Unlimited PTO Work? Learn the Pros and Cons." Bamboo HR. January 29, 2023. https://www.bamboohr.com/blog/benefits-limitations-unlimited-vacation

8. "Netflix Jobs: Work Life Balance." Netflix. Accessed June 22, 2023. https://jobs.netflix.com/work-life-philosophy

9. Ward, Marguerite." Unlimited vacation is a Scam Unless Managers Fight Burnout Culture." Insider. January 16, 2023. https://www.businessinsider.com/unlimited-pto-vacation-scam-time-off-managers-fight-burnout-culture-2023-1

10. Buck, Andrew. "15 Examples of Companies with Unlimited PTO in 2023." Flamingo. September 25, 2023. https://helloflamingo.com/companies-with-unlimited-pto/#:~:text=Kickstarter,much%20time%20off%20is%20acceptable

11. Interview with anonymous source. August 4th, 2019.

Chapter 26
Consistency vs. Flexibility

1. Legg, Timothy J. "What the Baader-Meinhoff Phenomenon Is and Why You May See It Again... and Again." Healthline. December 17, 2019. https://www.healthline.com/health/self-serving-bias

2. Dalai Lama Center for Peace and Education. "Dan Siegel: Name it to Tame it." YouTube. https://www.youtube.com/watch?v=ZcDLzppD4Jc

3. Skateboarding. "Help Save The Carlsbad Skatepark!." The Arena Media. October 13, 2004. https://www.skateboarding.com/news/help-save-the-carlsbad-skatepark

Chapter 27
Traditional HR vs. HR Evolutions

1. "New Hire Introductory Periods." Lynchburg Regional SHRM. March 26, 2018. https://lrshrm.shrm.org/blog/2018/03/new-hire-introductory-periods

2. United States Department of Labor. "Fact Sheet #71: Internship Programs Under the Fair Labor Standards Act." Wage and Hour Division. Modified January 2018. https://www.dol.gov/agencies/whd/fact-sheets/71-flsa-internships

Chapter 28
The Best Questions, Not the Best Answers

1. Maxwell, John C. *Good Leaders Ask Great Questions: Your Foundation for Successful Leadership*. New York, NY: Center Street, 2014.
2. NPR. "Stitch Fix's Katrina Lake at the How I Built This Summit," December 13, 2018. https://www.npr.org/2018/12/11/675886163/stitch-fixs-katrina-lake-at-the-hibt-summit

Chapter 29
Avoid Software Vendor Benders

1. "What is Salesforce?" Salesforce, Inc. Accessed May 7, 2023. https://www.salesforce.com/products/what-is-salesforce/

Chapter 30 Building an HR Team from Scratch

1. Indeed Editorial Team. "HR to Employee Ratio: A Definitive Guide." Indeed. Modified January 31, 2023. https://www.indeed.com/career-advice/career-development/hr-to-employee-ratio

Appendix

1. Pink, Daniel H. *To Sell Is Human: The Surprising Truth about Persuading, Convincing, and Influencing Others.* Canongate, 2018.